# GENE SIMMONS

# SEX MONEY KISS

SIMMONS BOOKS/NEW MILLENNIUM PRESS
*Beverly Hills*

## ALSO AVAILABLE FROM NEW MILLENNIUM:

*Kiss and Make-Up* 6 Cassettes-Unabridged .... $29.95

*Kiss and Make-Up* 8 CDs-Unabridged ........ $49.95

*Sex Money KISS* Limited Edition lunchbox .... $19.95

*Sex Money KISS* Limited Edition T-shirt ...... $19.95
 (Sizes M, L, XL, XXL)

*Sex Money KISS* Limited Edition lunchbox with
 audiobook CDs-Unabridged and bonus songs ... $49.95

Please send check or money order plus $5.00 per item to cover shipping and handling to:
 **Dept. SP, New Millennium Audio**
 **301 North Canon Drive, Suite 214, Beverly Hills, CA 90210**
Please make sure to enclose your name, mailing address and specify the items you wish to purchase.

Printed in the United States of America

ISBN: 1-893224-86-4

Library of Congress Cataloging-in-Publication Data Available

Design: Kerry DeAngelis, KL Design

Simmons Books/New Millennium Press
301 North Canon Drive, Suite 214
Beverly Hills, CA 90210

www.genesimmons.com
www.NewmillenniumPress.com

10 9 8 7 6 5 4 3 2 1

*To my mother, Flora,*
*who gave me life itself.*

# Who Am I?

Who am I, and why am I writing this book?

Let's face it, just because I stick out my tongue a lot and spit fire doesn't mean I have any qualifications to advise anyone on relationship, money or career issues.

I don't.

I've never been married. Yet I've been living with a gorgeous woman I'm crazy about for twenty years with never a cross word between us, in a relationship based on honesty and full disclosure. I never went to business school—I have a pedestrian understanding of commodities and futures, at best. Yet "expert financial people" work for me! I never had a grand master plan for my career; I graduated from college with a B.A. in education, fully prepared to work as a teacher. And yet for three decades I've been in KISS: a band that has broken every possible record—from album sales to merchandising and licensing to touring.

What I do have and have always had, thanks in full to my mother, is an abiding faith in me. Call it a "life philosophy": a philosophy about relationships, money (mine!) and happiness (mine again).

It works for me. It can work for you!

## Call it a "life philosophy": a philosophy about relationships, money (mine!) and happiness (mine again).

# I'd like to start this book with a personal salute to the modern woman.

Ever since our shared primordial past, men and women have been living very defined roles. The man hunted, killed and brought home the bacon. The woman stayed at home and was totally dependent on the man. In return for a cave (home) and food, she would "earn her keep" by repaying her partner with sex.

He never looked to her to be his hunting partner. She couldn't run as fast as he could. She also didn't have the hand-eye coordination to accurately throw a spear. Not to mention the fact that even if she could run as fast as a man and throw that spear accurately, she simply did not possess the necessary physical strength, since she was substantially smaller and weaker than he was, to make much of a dent in a Mastodon.

Everything has changed. Or so we think. Modern technology, on the surface, leveled the playing field. The Information Age no longer demands large muscles to succeed in survival. There are certainly women out there who can out-perform and out-earn their male counterparts. And to them, I tip my hat.

These women refuse to bow down to certain biological urges. They have a menstrual cycle every month, their hips are wider (hence the phrase "she's a broad"–as in broad hips) and their breasts are much larger. This doesn't take into account certain psychological concerns like the biological clock—which is to say, they worry daily that they will be fertile only so long. They *must* find a mate. The modern woman has, she thinks, overcome the biological burdens of being a woman and can go toe to toe with man, unencumbered by the worries and concerns of her female ancestors.

I contend that sooner or later even the modern woman will give in to her biological urges and want to have her own mate. She will demand that he cease all activities with any other females while he has a breath left in his body ("till death do us part"). And if they separate (get divorced) most of the women out there will expect him to pay her (often) half of his gross pre-tax dollars (it's the law of the land in many states). Finally, she will complain until he drops dead that he refuses to lift the toilet seat when he pees.

Again, I salute her. She is a testament that women can go out there and earn their own money (or, in the patois of our prehistoric past, "kill their own meat").

Please note, I am going to be painting with wide strokes in this book. When I say "men" it includes most men (actually, privately, I will tell you it includes almost all men without exception) and when I say "women" I mean to say most of these women in the United States (you know, the masses who watch soap operas, *Dr. Phil* and *Oprah*—I watch *Dr. Phil* as well, by the way) and certainly on the entire planet. "Women" does not necessarily include the "modern woman"—but I contend if you wait long enough, IT WILL!

Women make one or two eggs at a time and can conceive only through their middle years. Men, on the other hand, don't have menstrual cycles. Men don't have a biological clock (we never even think about it). Men ejaculate billions of sperm at a time. None of the sperm is lined up in a straight line pointed only at the woman who's in bed with him at the time. And the healthy, straight sexual male will be able to ejaculate billions more within a few minutes to an hour. He will continue to be able to make billions of sperm until he drops dead. And women keep wondering why men can't be monogamous. Please don't send me hate mail; take that point up with the grand designer: Mother Nature.

Here's a thought: If man was predisposed to being monogamous (biologically), his sexual activity would have been limited to the cave he lived in, without spreading his seed in every other cave he rested in as he hunted the migrating herds. Now, don't lose me here. So in the days before civilization, before language and culture, we lived in clans. A few people huddled in a cave. Isn't it true that if man was predisposed to being monogamous that within a generation or two humankind would have been cross-eyed and retarded? Isn't inbreeding unhealthy? Aren't purebred Dalmatian dogs dumb as a rock? Aren't mutts smart? If nature has given man billions of sperm every time he gets excited, doesn't that mean he is designed to have sex with as many females as possible before he drops dead? I'm not saying he should or should not, only pointing out, isn't that what nature intended?

# Women are from Mars. Men have penis.

It's no wonder women have been torturing men since the days we crawled out of our caves. Just kidding.

And maybe you can take a hint from that last comment— whatever I say, about anything, is meant only as food for thought. You (men and women alike) decide everything for yourselves. You—men—do you want to have sex with as many women as possible (preferably at the same time)? And you—women—do you want a man who will stay committed to you emotionally, sexually and in all other ways to become your soul partner to the exclusion of all other women? (Can you guess the answer?)...

Women are from Mars. Men have penis.

Keep reading.

# MEN AND WOMEN...IF

If you put a woman on a pedestal and try to protect her from
the rat race, you are a male chauvinist pig.
If you stay home and do the housework, you're a pansy.

If you work too hard, there is never any time for her.
If you don't work enough, you're a good-for-nothing bum.

If she has a boring repetitive job with low pay, it's exploitation.
If you have a boring repetitive job with low pay, you should get off
your rear and find something better.

If you get a promotion ahead of her, it's favoritism.
If she gets a job ahead of you, it's equal opportunity.

If you mention how nice she looks, it's sexual harassment.
If you keep quiet, it's male indifference.

If you cry, you are a wimp. If you don't, you are insensitive.

If you make a decision without consulting her, you are a chauvinist.
If she makes a decision without consulting you, she's a liberated woman.

If you ask her to do something she doesn't enjoy, that's domination.
If she asks you, it's a favor.

If you appreciate the female form and frilly underwear, you are a pervert.
If you don't, you are gay.

If you like a woman to shave her legs and keep in shape you are sexist.
If you don't, you are unromantic.

If you try to keep yourself in shape, you are vain.
If you don't, you are a slob.

If you buy her flowers, you are after something.
If you don't, you are not thoughtful.

If you're proud of your achievements, you are full of yourself.
If you're not, you have no ambition.

If she has a headache she is tired. If you have a headache, you're gay.

If you want it too often, you are oversexed. If you don't, you're gay.

This book is written in simple terms. You should find it easy to digest, clear in its intent and brutally honest. It's going to distill and demystify some of the institutions that Western society is built on. It is not a self-help book, a "relationship" book or a book of philosophy, theology or morality. It's not even a business book, per se. My philosophy isn't taught in business schools. This book doesn't use business language, which is designed for business school graduates. This is plain speak to understand plain notions. Its intent is to make sure on the day that you die, and certainly while you're living, you can have a lot more money in your pocket and maybe even be happier.

For that to happen, you're going to have to redraw some lines in the sand which have been drawn for you by other people, society, religion and convention...many of which are ancient and therefore archaic, in my opinion. And what gives me the right to redraw these lines (some of which are fundamental to the American way of life)? Who am I to espouse any of these notions?

I am living proof that the American dream is not only alive but alive and well, thank you. I've amassed cash, more of it than I ever thought possible. I graduated from college and taught sixth grade for a very short time. I worked as the assistant to the director of a government research and demonstration project, I worked at *Vogue* magazine as an assistant to the editor, and I worked as a Kelly Girl. I've also been a rock star for thirty years. But teacher or rock star, whatever I was doing to make a living, I was constantly living by the notions that I thought would increase my bottom line, while

> **I am living proof that the American dream is not only alive but alive and well, thank you.**

completely rejecting those notions (whether they were religious or social) that robbed me of what I thought belonged to me: MY CASH.

What will you say right before they put you six feet under? Will you say:

"I wish I would have."

"I wish I could have."

"I wish I should have..."

Or will you say, "I did it all. Thank you and good night."

# Ready? Let's get started.

# CHAPTER ONE

# The Choices Are Yours

**Y**ou've heard it all before. This time, *listen!!*

Waste not, want not.

A penny saved is a penny earned.

It's almost always the messenger and not so much the message. It's who says something, not so much what they're saying.

The vacuum cleaner salesman isn't really selling you vacuum cleaners. He's selling you himself. If you buy the salesman, you'll buy what he is selling. In religion, in politics, in love, in life!!

Once you learn that the most important commodity you possess is you, yourself, and no one else, you will probably make a lot more money!

I know I have. So can you.

But along the way, you will have to ignore and reject some of the "rules of society" your preacher, teacher and, yes, even mom and dad taught you. You will lose friends, but along the way you might wind up richer and happier.

It's your decision.

It always is!!

**Once you learn that the most important commodity you possess is you, yourself, and no one else, you will probably make a lot more money!**

# No Rules

You should take everything I say with a grain of salt. No matter what I say, or what graduates of any business school will tell you, the truth is that there are so many variables to almost anything and everything in this book (and almost any other book you will ever read about acquiring wealth) that there simply are no rules.

What you can do is take a look at your lifestyle. Even if you don't change your career or reinvent yourself, you can make an enormous increase in the amount of your net dollars, much more than you will by following the paint-by-numbers rules of this 21st century Western culture. You've got to think outside the box, and you've got to break rules, traditions and certain philosophical and perhaps religious morals you've been taught. Because morals are relative, and morals, along with ethics, rituals and social customs, cost a lot of money. Ultimately, that's the bottom line. That's not just a phrase I'm using here to make it sound flowery. Bottom line means bottom line. *Cash.* Even once you earn the money and once you pay your taxes, I will show you how you can have more in your pocket as opposed to less.

Before I get into this any further, I've had discussions with people who are more "spiritual" than I will ever admit to being. I've always found "spiritual" akin to watching *Casper the Friendly Ghost* cartoons. I've yet to have someone explain to my satisfaction exactly what "spiritual" means. I'm assuming it means, "I'm a nice person." Well, I suppose we all have that side to our personality, but to me "spiritual" brings up images of crystals, horoscopes, numerology and nut-jobs. I speak in plain language to espouse my philosophy, which is that while I'm alive I want to enjoy myself, and the way to enjoy myself is to have a lot of money. Money is the key that unlocks everything: sex, happiness and taking care of the ones I love by feeding them, sheltering them, giving them medical treatments if needed, ad infinitum. Money buys what, unfortunately, love can't.

That's a shocking thing to understand if you've grown up in our culture, which has taught us that "love is all." Love...be all, love all. It's a load of nonsense, actually, because even though it would be very nice if that was in fact the case, the harsh reality is that it's not. If you want to get

**While I'm alive I want to enjoy myself, and the way to enjoy myself is to have a lot of money. Money is the key that unlocks everything: sex, happiness, and taking care of the ones I love.**

on the bus to get across the city, you can't smile at the bus driver and say, "I love you. Can I have a seat?" He's still going to want cash to let you on the bus. If that bus driver hates you, and you give him the right amount of cash, he'll still give you a ride. And that's what this book is all about. We have to figure out "the bus ride of life." In order for that to happen, you need cash, baby. That, by the way, is a good use of the word "baby..." Emphasis!!

But back to spirituality. The spiritual people out there will say to me, "I'm not like you. Cash is not the most important thing to me." To that I offer this, and you be the judge: God appears in a cloud of smoke, poof! He's right there in your bedroom. (For those of you who believe God should be a female, let it be so! God's a she.) And he/she/it says to you, "Hey, it's me, God. Listen, no one's around. You know that wallet you have in your pocket? I'm going to give you a choice: You can have one or the other, not both. No matter how much money you have in your wallet, I'm going to give you a chance to either have more or less in that wallet of yours. You must pick one or the other. Which will it be?"

I am convinced that those among us who are sane can only choose MORE. If you choose less, you are either 1) insane or 2) lying (to me, yourself and everybody else). Life has always been and will always be about the pursuit of more. The word MORE should be one of the most admired words in the English language. But in fact we've been taught by politically correct people that the word "more" has negative connotations. People run around saying, "I don't want more stuff." That's a lie. Don't ever believe them. Because when anybody wins the lottery and gets $100 million in their pockets, they (along with you, I, my mother, your grandmother, my gardener and everybody else in the world) will have pieces of meat flying out of their throats as they scream "Whoop de fucking doo!" Why? Because they suddenly have so much MORE. More cash, and lots of it, baby. There's that word again I love so much: *baby*, for emphasis.

> Life has always been and will always be about **the pursuit of more.** The word **MORE** should be one of the most admired words in the English language.

Don't live the lie. Be clear, be truthful. Stand there proudly, unapologetically, unabashedly and say, "I love cash. It will get me everything I want in life." Understand it and believe it, even though you'll get furrowed eyebrows and disapproving looks from people who will tell you, "Money isn't everything." They are actually incorrect. It *is* everything. If your mother is sick and you love her, only cash will buy her medicine. Your child is hungry, you love your child; only cash will buy your child food. Love will unfortunately do very little. A crook is about to rob you and points a gun in your face. Your life is in danger. You could tell him you love him, try the Jesus path. The same thing will happen to you that happened to Him. You'll get crucified, and you don't even have to be a Jew like He was. I suggest you try this one instead: Offer him cash. You might live. Here is how your chance of staying alive will increase: Offer him *more* (cash, that is) and just keep on offering more. The word MORE will buy God himself. Even He likes it when the hat is passed around.

So the faster you become comfortable with the notion that cash is good and more cash is even better, the faster you'll understand that *any person*, institution or notion that tries to take your cash is your enemy. And unless you are either 1) insane or 2) delusional, you should do everything in your power to prevent those enemies from taking your cash. Because cash will help you survive and do whatever you want to do. And better my cash in my pocket than in yours, baby.

I'm assuming no one wants to walk through a jungle with their eyes closed. It makes your chances for survival minimal, at best. You want to keep your eyes completely open to increase your chances of survival. The tools you have are your five senses, plus your intellect. Likewise, those are the same tools that will enable

> Don't live the lie. Be clear, be truthful. Stand there proudly, unapologetically, unabashedly, and say, "I love cash. It will get me everything I want in life."

you to make more money. Anyone and everything—institutions, religion, your girlfriend, your mother—who mutes or in other ways dilutes those tools is your enemy, sad to say. Your enemy—because they minimize your chances of making more money.

This is also why drugs and alcohol are your enemy: because they will rob you of more than one of your senses. They will rob you of the ability to see straight, think straight or even be conscious. Never mind the cost and repercussions, domino-effect-wise, of paying for all those habits.

Winners, despite what we've all been told, don't have square jaws and are not the biggest guys around. They are just like you and me. They don't have to be born in America; they can have funny last names. I certainly had one. I came to America when I was nine and couldn't speak English until I was in my early teens. I had a funny name and a funny accent, and I knew nothing about my new country. All I knew was that although I might be the object of derision, no one tried to kill me. And therein lies the great blessing of America: You can try anything you want, as many times as you like, and no one will stop you. You will not be arrested by the government and otherwise incarcerated for saying or doing almost anything. That includes making porno films. Yes, you can even do that and make a fortune.

> **Winners, despite what we've all been told, don't have square jaws and are not the biggest guys around. They are just like you and me.**

Your work is your friend. It makes you money.

Your boss is your friend. He might give you more money.

You are your own best friend. If you don't want to go out there and work for the money, who will?

I like the idea of the American tax system. I may grumble along with everyone else about the amount I have to give to the government, but by and large I find it a fair trade. In return for my tax dollars I get nuclear armed forces, a highway system, police and fire protection...an infrastructure that's available no place else on earth. And again, they (the government) don't butt into my busi-ness. If I want to do almost anything, by and large they stay out of it. They do encour-age me to go out and make more money, so they can get more tax dollars from me. That's a good, healthy rela-tionship.

> You are your own best friend. If you don't want to go out there and work for the money, **who will?**

You can completely disre-gard everything I say, because there are lots of other books that will take you through the tried and true (they say) methods of acquir-ing wealth. Or you can watch late-night television and see real estate experts who will tell you how, for "no money down," you can acquire real estate and eventually make your fortune, if only you send away for their tapes! I applaud men like them or almost any-one else who figures out a way to (hold your breath) get *your* cash in *their* pocket. And don't forget more, baby. I'm not judging whether what they have to say is either good, bad, true or untrue. It simply means that they've figured out a way (again, if you haven't been paying attention) to get *your* cash in *their* pocket, and that's what life is about.

God has given me two pockets: one on the right side and one on the left side. And there is only one way to look at cash. It's either coming in or going out. Just like mail on your desk—there's an "in" box and an "out" box. That's the cornerstone of all com-merce: imports and exports. What you want is to have fewer imports and more exports. You want *them* to buy more of *your* stuff than you do of their stuff. I apologize for diverting for a second into the international economics of commerce, but the same ideas apply to you and me. The same rules will always apply and always have. I'd better be making more than I spend, or I'll be asking you if you want fries with that. If you understand these notions, then maybe I'm the guy who will give you a good solid kick in the butt. Because boy, do you need it. You've been fooled by convention, by ritual and by the social quagmire we all swim in. It's thick soup, and it is riddled and populated (please don't consider this judgmental) by followers, not leaders. If you think for yourself, you will make very few friends. But you might make a lot more cash...*baby!!!*

> **If you think for yourself, you will make very few friends. But you might make a lot more cash...*baby!!!***

There are certain universal truths. Everybody wants more money and nobody wants to get run over by a truck. Given those facts, it's shocking how often people cross the street without looking both ways. Instead of deciding to go to Wharton Business School to increase your chances of making more money, if people would simply look both ways, cross at the green instead of against the light and do all the other commonsense things we were taught as children, at the very least they would save enormous amounts of money. Not only will running into traffic get you hit by a truck, it will cost you money when you lose time from work recovering. It will also cost you a lot to get fixed up at the hospital, just so you can return to work to make more money.

Let me put it another way, as plainly as I can. If there's one big "don't" in life it's this: Don't dive into the deep end of the pool if you don't know how to swim. Never (or not until you're filthy rich—$100 million). Life isn't about taking chances—not for you and not for me. Granted, that's an unromantic notion, because the tendency for almost everyone while they're young is to feel invulnerable, that nothing can stop you.

I won't belabor some of the other "don'ts"—don't smoke, don't drink, don't get high, because people seem to need those crutches, and will fight anyone who tries to make them stop. Here's another: Don't pay to pray. If you're religious, by all means go to church, but don't give them all your money. If you want to tithe, 10 percent of your gross pre-tax dollars winds up being about 20 percent of net (at the highest tax rate). That's a lot of money out of your pockets into theirs.

I've never liked that tradition in churches and synagogues of passing the hat. I don't want to give God any money. It reminds me of an old joke. A rabbi and a priest are talking. The priest says to the rabbi, "We are men of God," and the rabbi agrees, "Yes, you are right." "But Rabbi," the priest says, "I notice you have a big wad of cash in your pocket. Where did you get all that money?" The rabbi replies, "Oh, in my temple, after I give a sermon we pass the hat. Don't you?" "Of course," says the priest, "after I preach we pass the hat. But I give my money to God, don't you?" The rabbi says, "Of course! I take the hatful of cash and throw it up to heaven. And whatever God doesn't want, I keep."

Give to Caesar what is Caesar's. If God needs a handout, have him ask some other sucker!

> **If there's one big "don't" in life it's this: *Don't dive into the deep end of the pool if you don't know how to swim.* Never (or not until you're filthy rich—$100 million). Life isn't about taking chances— not for you and not for me.**

The Bible also says (if you study theology on any other level beyond going to church and, lemminglike, repeating words and phrases you have no clue about), "Do not petition thy Lord with prayer." By the way, petition means asking for stuff, including cash. It says so right in the holy books.

When you live according to the "rules" of religion and marriage, God will be happy because he's getting his slice in church (tax-free). Your wife is going to be thrilled after your divorce because she's going to get her slice: *half*. That's half of everything you've got! What do *you* get? Remember, you're the guy making the money. You get zip. And for those women to whom the opposite applies—he may get *your* money—same thing.

*I have lived by my own philosophies from my earliest childhood days. In the following pages I will tell you more about my life and how this way of thinking brought me all the sex, money and KISS anyone could dream of. This is what I did and how I did it…and here's the big secret: You can do it too.*

# CHAPTER TWO

# Early Lessons

I learned very early in life to act in a fiduciary (dictionary definition: "relating to or involving confidence or trust") manner. But it really means I have a responsibility—in this case to myself—to make more money, not less. In case you haven't read my *New York Times* bestseller *Kiss and Make-Up*, you may not be aware that first and foremost, I was not born in America, the land of opportunity. I was born in Israel on August 25, 1949, about six months after the country survived a war of independence. Times were hard.

But the interesting thing about those hard times is that I was completely oblivious to them. I never went hungry. And that's one of the real lessons to keep in your mind. When the stock market crashed in America in 1929 many people lost enormous fortunes. It was the single largest loss of U.S. dollars in American history. People who were otherwise relatively young and healthy, who had been multimillionaires, didn't think twice about going to the windows of skyscrapers and jumping to their deaths, because this big idea—their money/dollars—had disappeared.

But consider this: In order to survive, you don't need a lot. If you're not starving, you're surviving. You're successful at being alive. Above and beyond that, it's up to

**If you're not starving, you're surviving. You're successful at being alive. Above and beyond that, it's up to each person to decide what makes them happy.**

each person to decide what makes them happy. My contention is that if you're happy with the bare necessities, the little things, you're in the game. You will *always* have another chance to make more money. Remember, this is America. And don't kid yourself, it *is* about *more* money.

Once you gamble from a position of strength, which is to say you're alive and you've got enough to eat, you have all the tools you need to go out there and grab your piece of the pie. Hell, go for the whole pie! That's always been my philosophy. Even though I've done well for myself, it's still the small things in life that give me the most pleasure. A good piece of Danish is more satisfying, by far, than gargling with 100-year-old wine.

When I was a little boy in Israel, I wasn't aware that I was poor. I came from a broken home. My mother was the sole breadwinner. There were no brothers or sisters, so I had a lot of time to myself. And I learned from the very beginning of my life that if I didn't make myself happy, no one else would. My mother would supply the basics—food and shelter—but it was up to me to make myself happy. So in the same way that the children of Israel in biblical times wandered through the desert starving to death, once manna (food) came from heaven, the Promised Land was beside the point, at least for the moment. As long as you have manna and a place to sleep, whether you get to the Promised Land or not doesn't matter. You're surviving. If you're surviving, eventually you'll get to the Promised Land. As a little boy, I always had enough to eat, and because of that I had no doubts I would get to the Promised Land.

My mother was a Jewess from Hungary who had survived the German Nazi concentration camps of World War II. Her perspective, coming from the camps and landing in Israel, was that she had arrived in the land of plenty. At least no one was trying to kill her! It's all perspective.

As a young boy of six I wanted to show my mother that I loved

They say the apple doesn't fall far from the tree. If that's true, I am certainly the son of my mother. She was born Flora Klein in Jand, Hungary, in 1927. She was barely fourteen years old when the entire German nation became insane and took to heart the words of a failed painter, Adolf Hitler.

Lest we become too politically correct here, let me say in no uncertain terms that the German people of the 1930s and '40s were to blame for what was to become World War II and the Holocaust. For those of you who haven't read much about it, this much is undisputed historical fact: About 6 million European Jews were incinerated in the ovens of the concentration camps. But that number didn't include the 2 million Catholics, 2 million gay men and 2 million Gypsies who were also wiped out. The war itself is said to have reduced the world's entire population by close to 100 million people. Of those, 20 million were Russians.

Fourteen-year-old Flora Klein stood there as her mother walked her own mother into the gas chamber. She later explained to me that her mother didn't want her own mother to face death alone.

My mother survived the camps because she had gone to beauty school and had some hairstyling and make-up skills. The commandant's wife took a liking to her, and because my mother provided the wife with beauty tips, my mother was able to survive by eating scraps.

The end of World War II came about when America, God bless her, entered the war and along with its allies, ended the madness. My mother soon met my father, Jechiel Witz. He was the tallest in his village and was considered a catch by all the girls. They soon married and in 1949 moved to Israel, just a few months after it had become an independent country.

Here is my mother in a photo taken in Israel. My mother is not an educated woman. She has never traveled the world. She is a survivor, from a time when very few people lived through the Holocaust. But she was then, and continues to be now, my inspiration. Through her eyes, I have seen only the possibilities of everything in life. I have learned to believe that all glasses are half full and not half empty. Through her heart, I have learned that although man was capable of unimaginable inhumanity, there was still good in the world. She has always instilled in me a fearless backbone. "Reach for the stars," she would tell me.

I am, admittedly, self-absorbed. I am also self-motivated and relentless in my pursuits. I am also delusional about how good or how good-looking I actually am, which may have helped me through the years.

But everything I am, I owe to my Dear Mother. Without her, I would be nothing.

INSPIRATION

I was born on August the 25th, 1949, in Haifa, Israel.

When I was a little boy (in this photo, I'm about three years old), my mother expected me to do my best and would settle for nothing less. Even today, after I proudly report to her about my new ventures, she tells me how proud she is of me.

And then she asks me what else I'm working on.

her. I wanted to give her money—and to get money, I had to earn it. So I went up into the hills of Mt. Carmel, where I lived in Israel, and picked cactus fruit that grew wild in the hills. Cactus fruit has prickles all over it on the outside and is very sweet on the inside, perhaps an apt analogy for who and what I am. Israelis are called *Sabras*. "Sabra" is the Hebrew word for cactus fruit.

I picked the cactus fruit and asked someone how to get rid of the thorns on the outside. I learned that you floated the cactus fruit in a tub of cold water with ice in it. I hauled a big metallic tub of ice water filled with cactus fruit down to the bus station. I was waiting there when the bus arrived filled with tired workers coming home from a long day on the job. The bus station was on a dirt road. Paved roads were mostly unknown in the Israel of the early fifties.

I made a killing selling cactus fruit to the workers. Each cactus fruit sold for a *prutah* (half a penny). And I made enough money to buy myself a nice lunch—beans and rice, which I always loved. I brought the rest of the money I'd earned that day back home and put it on the table for my mother. And I will never forget it made her cry. It was then I understood the connection between making money and giving it to someone as a way of showing your love. No matter how much I told my mother I loved her, it was the work put in and the money earned that elicited that response.

When we first arrived in America I realized that there were no vistas that couldn't be reached, a double negative which means: You *can* have anything you want. And the fewer partners you have in your life, the more you'll be able to keep for yourself. Certain things in life are a given—death and taxes among them—and since everything costs something, the idea by and large is to avoid anything you don't find necessary in your life so you can have more for yourself. Money, that is.

The first job I had in America was working after school as a butcher's assistant in Brooklyn, New York. I must have been nine-and-a-half years old. I scrubbed the fat off of the chopping block so that bacteria wouldn't collect there. It was very important that the chopping block stay sanitized so all the meat the butcher cut throughout the day wouldn't be tainted. I frequently had to go down into the basement to bring up fresh meat, and every time I descended the stairs I heard the pitter-patter of little feet running back into the shadows. No matter how disgusting that job was, and no matter how much I disliked going to that butcher shop every day, I was positively thrilled at the prospect of receiving a lot of money (by my standards) at the end of each week.

As in Israel, when I got the money, which in those days amounted to $15 a week, I put a little bit aside to buy my comic books and bubble gum. The rest I would give to my mother. She would say things like, "That's my big man." Inferences in language reflect Western culture's ideal of the man who goes out and brings home the money—the "provider." Even though in point of fact my mother was the only one who

> # I never believed in luck. The harder I worked, the luckier I got.

brought home money. *She* was my role model. Seeing the world through her eyes, I never believed in luck. The harder I worked, the luckier I got.

My mother had a true blue-collar "workingman's" ethic. After her divorce, she never looked to anyone else to put food on the table. She rolled up her sleeves and went to work herself. She was a great beauty in her youth, and it would have been easy for her to remarry. But she devoted herself to my upbringing. Whenever I've spoken with my mother about why it is she and my father got divorced, she has always been very clear. "He didn't know how to be successful." "He didn't know how to earn a living." "He was not a good provider." Inference: he didn't bring home the money. He didn't! The same inference, by the way, doesn't apply to women— i.e, whether or not she's a "good provider." It didn't apply then, and it doesn't today.

# Cheap

**Pennies are everything. The more pennies you have, the more dollars you have.**

I remember when I was about twelve years old I had a friend in school who used to call me "cheap." Two or three of us would be on our way to the schoolyard to play, and this friend would tell the other guys in our group that I was willing to chase a penny if he threw it on the ground. I was a "penny-pincher" or a "penny-chaser," he would say. To demonstrate, he would take a penny out of his pocket and throw it. I would obligingly go and pick it up and put it in my pocket. Every once in a while a nickel would follow, and I'd scoop that up and put it in my pocket too. I didn't think about these incidents for many years, until as time went on I heard the cliché—which I never considered a racial slur but a point of pride—that Jews were penny-pinchers. I thought it was a bizarre idea that there were actually people who *didn't* appreciate the value of a penny. It's OK for Benjamin Franklin, one of the founding fathers of our country, to be a penny-pincher (remember "a penny saved is a penny earned"). But it's not OK for a Jew or anyone else to be concerned about pennies?

Do not think the way "they" do. "They" are wrong. Pennies are everything. The more pennies you have, the more dollars you have. If you lose one dollar, you lose a lot of pennies. But if you save up lots of pennies, you'll certainly accumulate dollars. When buying or doing anything that costs more rather than less, you should be concerned. If you want to buy something you don't need, you should be concerned. If someone else wants your money, whether you're getting married or going out on a date with a girl who "expects" you to pay because that's the society we live in, you should be concerned. Don't take her to a movie. Don't take her out to dinner. Offer to come over to her apartment, or she can come over to yours. You'll have a much better chance of getting to the honeypot in a more private setting than spending lots of money just to find out you're not getting any at the end of the night. She may even prefer it that way. It's not always about lavishing money on a girl. And if it is, you better find out sooner than later. Remember, there are always other girls, but there isn't always another dollar.

> **Remember, there are always other girls, but there isn't always another dollar.**

Harsh notions, you say? Get ready. Here's more: The word "cheap" is a wonderful word! Learn to love it. Be cheap, just like me. And try this on for size: Less is more. That's right. If you want more, try having less. The less you spend, the more you have. That makes sense. We all know that. The less you smoke, the more you live. Well, that makes sense too, but we don't need to read it on the side of a cigarette pack. Or do we? We keep smoking anyway. It will cost you a fortune. And that doesn't take into account the cost of your future medical bills (remember cancer?) The less you complain, the happier you are. Perhaps. And tread lightly on this one: The less you marry, whether it's once or multiple times, the richer you are and

> **The word "cheap" is a wonderful word! Learn to love it. Be cheap, just like me.**

will be. And, of course, the less you eat, the thinner you are.

Why is it that when you tell a man there are three hundred billion stars in the universe he'll believe you. But when you tell him a bench has wet paint, he has to actually touch it to be sure. Why are the small things, the naked truths that stare us all in the face, the ones that are so hard to believe?

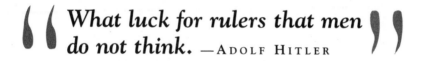

**Why** are the small things, the naked truths that **stare us all in the face,** the ones that are **so hard to believe?**

*" What luck for rulers that men do not think. —*ADOLF HITLER *"*

# The Fab Four

A pivotal point in my life occurred when I was about thirteen years old. *The Ed Sullivan Show,* a variety show popular in the 1960s, featured the Beatles performing in America for the first time. Even though I've often talked about how greatly that single event affected me, in retrospect it takes on more and more meaning in my life. It showed me, and perhaps I can show you, that certain events in your lifetime are "signposts" of a sort. We should all take heed, because they can, in a very real way, point us in the right direction. That last sentence was a bit on the poetic side, but it actually means something.

After I saw the Beatles I became inspired to do the same thing.

Not just for the purist notion of making the music itself, because that's not what it's really all about anyway (and any rock star who tells you he wanted to be in a band just to write and play his own music is lying). I was always honest with myself; I realized that the reason it would be fun to have my own band like the Beatles was that maybe I could get the girls to scream for me too. I didn't understand the money part of it back then, but it was clear, even at age thirteen, that being a Beatle was a pretty good job. I wished I could be one of them.

You can beg, borrow and hopefully not steal amplifiers and guitars. My mother, bless her, never took my rock-and-roll band or my comic books too seriously, but she figured they were the lesser of two evils. Either she indulged me in these hobbies or, she supposed, the alternative was my loitering on street corners and picking up all the other bad habits my friends were engaging in: hanging out, getting in trouble, booze, eventually drugs. My hobbies were certainly healthier outlets.

Like most people, we weren't rich. Every penny and every dollar counted. My mother couldn't afford to buy me an expensive bass guitar, but she did scrounge up $35 to buy me a secondhand Kent, which was a very cheap Japanese-made bass guitar made to look like Paul McCartney's Hofner. I didn't know the difference and didn't care. My mother didn't have enough money to buy me a bass amplifier either. So my friends and I found an old television set that someone had dumped. We brought the set up to my mother's apartment, tore out the insides, left the cabinet intact, went out and bought a big fifteen-inch bass speaker and in essence constructed our own amplifier. It was big by the day's standards. Size counted—even then.

In short order I joined my then-best friends Seth Dogramajian and Danny Haber, and we formed the Lynx. But at the school auditorium where they introduced us on our maiden voyage we were heralded as "The Missing Links," and the new name stuck. We played small parties and not only got more girls but were also paid money. The original sums we earned weren't much—I think we walked away with $25 to $50 per man after one of these shows— but you'd have to work a whole week in a butcher shop or delivering newspapers to get $50. It was an enormous amount of money to earn in one night. You could either work after school for a full week at a job you hated, or be in a rock band, get girls and earn the same amount of money!

I did both. I delivered newspapers—in fact, I had two newspaper routes—and played in a rock-and-roll band. I also went to school and published my own science fiction journal. I was also in the school chorus and in the school's drama club and worked on the school newspaper. My life was full then; it's full now. I didn't

## The lesson I learned then was that one can make things happen, even if one has no money.

know it back then, but the things I was doing then really apply to what I do now, and, more importantly, should apply to you as you read this. There's no reason on earth why you can't work at your job, go out in the evening, and also work at your hobby (hopefully more than one hobby). The lesson I learned then was that one can make things happen, even if one has no money.

It was around this time I joined Junior Achievement, a group for kids aged thirteen to fifteen. I learned more about corporate America and the capitalist system than I ever had in school. We met at the YMCA. We broke off into three or four different groups, and each group created its own business. We started with a business plan. Once we had agreed on the product, each of us had to go out

and raise capital (money) by knocking on doors and selling "shares" in a new venture. One company made cookies; another made napkins with insignias, and so on. The actual process of doing it hands-on made me understand viscerally the nature of business.

Getting back to my band, I eventually disbanded The Missing Links and formed a better one called The Long Island Sounds. As the band got better, the girls got better looking and the pay improved. They seem to go hand in hand: As your product improves, so does the demand and the more money you make! The more demand, the more you can increase your supply. The more popular the band became, the more people came to see us, the more money we made and the more girls we got. Ants are attracted to picnics. More ants are attracted to bigger picnics.

> As the band got **better**, the girls got better looking and the pay improved. They seem to go hand in hand: As your product improves, so does the demand and the **more money you make!**

I was all of fourteen years of age, and I was learning the basic tenets of the capitalist system. Supply and demand weren't just words in textbooks. It was clear to me that the less I spent, the more I had. And, the more everybody else spent on me, the more I had.

One of the cornerstones of Wall Street is "Buy low, sell high." What that means is you should buy when the price of a stock or commodities is low, if it still has value. Ideally, and if you're lucky, you should only sell when that price has gone up...way up. Buy low, sell high. Unfortunately the capitalist system is based

In 1966 I was fifteen years old. I was in a band called The Long Island Sounds. I had just learned to play the bass guitar (notice I'm looking down at the frets—don't wanna make a mistake), because I noticed everyone wanted to play regular guitar and that few guys wanted to learn to play bass. I figured, and rightfully so, there would be less competition and thus my services would be more highly valued.

I initially sang co-lead vocals with my school chum, Seth Dogramajian, who has unfortunately passed on but with the addition of my bass-playing duties, I was a double threat.

Here we are playing at a Country Club in Queens, New York. The bass guitar I'm holding was a $35 Japanese copy of a bass guitar called the Hofner Bass, which Paul McCartney played in the Beatles. Needless to say, I wanted to be in the Beatles. We all did. And if there were no positions open, at least I could have a Hofner-style bass.

We lugged our own gear into station wagons. We were too young to drive, so one of our parents would usually drive us. We made sure no one saw the parents drive us up. Not cool. We would play the three sets and, at the end of the night, collect $150. We had very few expenses, and that meant we would each walk away with about $30 to $40. A huge sum in those days. I would have to work an entire week at my after school newspaper delivery route to earn that much. Here I was actually enjoying what I was doing, flirting with girls and looking cool (notice my polka-dot shirt), working (if you could call it that) for about three hours and still making the equivalent of what I would otherwise be making working an entire week. It was a revelation.

Incidentally, I continued to hold down my newspaper delivery routes (I had two—so I could make twice the amount) and play with the band on the weekends. I was clearing about $100 a week. I hardly ever took girls to movies and lavished hot dogs and popcorn on them. I would usually go over to their houses, let THEM feed ME, watch their television and have complete privacy, while their parents were away, to do as I pleased...with their daughter. I could have fun with girls AND keep my $100-a-week pay.

Life was good.

on the notion that at some point somebody else's misfortune will become your fortune. But it doesn't have to be that black-and-white. A win-win situation is when somebody is glad to give you money for their perception of its value.

There is no such thing as the "value of things." There is only the *perceived* value of things. Diamonds are valuable only because we all agree they are. I can get up on stage, wiggle my tongue and throw up blood as part of KISS and make lots of money for doing it, but only because people agree that what I do has value.

Playing in The Long Island Sounds was a lot of fun, and while it actually made me some money, it really provided me a canvas against which I learned some very important lessons. I would put these lessons to full use when the real thing happened: KISS.

But back then I was going to school until 3:00 in the afternoon. By about 4:00 I'd start my newspaper routes and finish by 5:30. I'd go home and do my homework. If I had any time left I'd work on my fan magazines ("fanzines"), which, strangely enough, also increased my popularity in school.

People were fascinated by these home-published fanzines. I was always interested in science fiction, fantasy, horror... anything that was free from the restrictions and limitations of real life. Superman flew through the air and defied gravity; King Kong was larger than life, Dr. Frankenstein's Monster was

> There is no such thing as the "value of things." There is only the *perceived* value of things. Diamonds are valuable only because we all agree they are. I can get up on stage, wiggle my tongue and throw up blood as part of KISS and make lots of money for doing it, but only because people agree that what I do has value.

-KLEIN-

I used to be Gene Klein. When I came to America, I assumed my mother's maiden name, Klein. At age fourteen, I was completely immersed in science fiction and fantasy. I read voraciously: Famous Monsters of Filmland and Castle of Frankenstein magazines, Analog and Amazing Stories monthly, comic books and books. I discovered an "underground press" of fans who published their own fan magazines, known as "fanzines." I started writing and drawing for these fanzines and eventually would go on to publish, write and edit my own fanzines. The first one was Adventure. Others would follow: Cosmos, Faun, Tinderbox and Cosmostiletto (when my fanzine merged with Stiletto, another fanzine).

Fans exchanged letters of comment ("LOCs") and made copies of our fanzines available to each other for either a small cover price (25 to 50 cents) or a LOC. LOCs were usually preferred. The fanzines were not money makers, but they were terrific on-the-job experience. You learned by doing. You learned about supply and demand. You learned what the cost of supplies was. And you learned how to be a better artist, designer, editor and publisher. This is my cover art for another fanzine called Fantasy News. I saw a Gil (Green Lantern) Kane comic book with a T-Rex in it and loved his version of the dinosaur so much, I tried doing my own version. The fellow at the upper right hand corner was an illustration I started and soon abandoned in favor of doing the T-Rex. Year of the art: 1964.

made up of dead people. They were all about breaking the rules. Not knowing a single thing about publishing, I decided to write, edit and publish science fiction/fantasy fan magazines, called fanzines. Some of the titles were *Cosmos*, *Faun*, and *Tinderbox*. My mother had been kind enough to buy me a Rexograph (hectograph) machine, then a mimeograph machine and finally a cheap photocopier. I charged twenty-five cents for each fanzine. They were not money makers, but it was great hands-on experience for a novice—the actual process of creating something, producing it and trying to figure out how to sell it.

By early evening I could eat dinner, spend time with my mother, watch a little television and even flirt with girls on the phone. Every day was full. Around this time I started fiddling with writing songs of my own. They were terrible of course, but I used to play them for my friends, who were fascinated that I had actually written them. They thought I had copied somebody else's song and was now playing it for them. I assured them that I had made up my own words and my own melody.

On the weekends I played baseball, rehearsed with the band in the afternoon, delivered my newspapers, and collected my weekly newspaper salary of anywhere between $15 to $50 a week. Then, if

Number 3    FEBRUARY ISSUE    price: a LOC

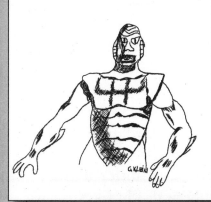

G.KLEIN

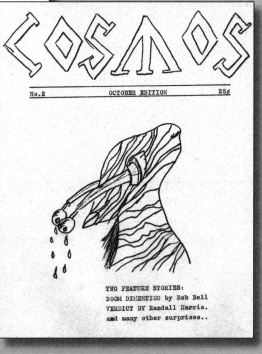

No.2    OCTOBER EDITION    25¢

TWO FEATURE STORIES:
DOOM DIMENTION by Bob Bell
VERDICT BY Randall Harris.
and many other surprises..

Cosmos *(before Carl Sagan used the title)* was another one of my fanzines. I would hand draw the different logos and cover artwork on carbon paper (which could only make three copies), then I would redraw the art on another carbon and so on, until I "published" about fifteen copies. That was the beginning of my publishing experience. We couldn't afford for a fourteen-year-old boy to have a hobby that incurred publishing expenses. The total cost of drawing and typing *Cosmos* was probably under $10 per issue.

Eventually my mother bought me a hectograph (or Rexograph) reproducing machine and then a mimeograph machine (pour ink into the drum, move it around with a paint brush, attach your stencil and the ink would ooze through the typewritten pages onto the printed page).

The bug-eyed fellow on the cover of Issue No. 2 was a creation of mine. The contents were either written by me or other sci-fi fans. The third issue features my drawing of the Creature From The Black Lagoon, *one of my favorite movies.*

People think that a fourteen-year-old boy fooling around with science fiction and editing a fanzine doesn't really have an application in the real world. They're wrong. I now have my own magazine, GENE SIMMONS TONGUE. And it's a direct result of my experiences publishing my fanzine as a young teenager.

Everything you do when you're living at home as a child has a direct cause and effect when you grow up. What you do as a hobby could very well be what makes you money as a grown-up.

I was lucky, The Long Island Sounds would have two gigs (shows), which would make me another $100 to $200 richer. By my standards, I was amassing a small fortune in no time at all, while still having enough time to go to school, deliver newspapers, be in a rock-and-roll band, flirt with girls, watch TV and make more money having fun than I would at normal jobs I hated.

> **If the week consists of seven days, there's no reason in the world why you shouldn't fill up every one of those days. "You snooze, you lose" isn't just a cliché.**

This is a very important idea, one I will probably refer to again: If the week consists of seven days, there's no reason in the world why you shouldn't fill up every one of those days. "You snooze, you lose" isn't just a cliché. The choices on weekends are watching football on television, where guys on one team (all dressed alike with numbers on their backs) go running against other guys on the other team (all dressed alike with more numbers on their backs) or working through the day (making more money) and still having the evening to do with as you please.

# Time Is Money

Time is money. I mean it! We've all heard this one before. But it's true. We even use variations of the phrase as clichés, as in, "Don't waste my time." But they're true!

To crystallize this idea for you, I'd like to offer the following snippet my friend Rich Abramson told me. His high school teacher asked one of the students to stand in front of the class. He gave the kid a dollar and asked him to look at the clock on the wall, make note of the time and then tear the dollar into little bits. The kid hesitated, then did as he was instructed. It was 10:16 in the morning and the dollar was in little bits. Now what?

The teacher said, "Notice the time? 10:16? You will never have that minute back, ever again. But that dollar? You can always make more dollars."

Get rid of things that take up too much of your time...especially those things that don't make you money. Get rid of people in your life who loaf. They will draw you in and suck up your precious time. Let your couch potato friend watch the ball game alone. Let your girlfriend go window shopping with someone else. You have better things to do with your time. Like making money.

> **Get rid of things that take up too much of your time...especially those things that don't make you money.**

Plenty of people have a "don't worry about it" philosophy. "I have lots of time. I'll do it. One day." It's foolhardy. Let's pause for a moment. If we're lucky, we live an average life span of about seventy years. About half of that is spent unconscious, sleeping. That leaves us with approximately thirty-five years of life. A full two weeks, we are told, is spent simply waiting for the light to turn green, just so we can cross the street. During that time we're helpless, doing nothing, waiting on a street corner. I would imagine we spend a year and a half or so of our lives (if we live in big cities) just waiting for elevators to take us to our floors. Let's not go into the months of sitting on the toilet and, God forbid, adding up the years we spend in our cars, going to and from work, vacation, you name it. Subtract years off your remaining thirty-five years.

So how much time do we actually have in life? Real life, with choices? Again, it's up to you to decide for yourself what you want to do with the remaining time you have left. You have to deduct as many as twenty years, because we're babies, then teenagers, then young adults, where the rules are decided for us. Mom and Dad tell you where to go and what to do. In school they tell you what homework to do and what time to show up. You have very few choices the first twenty years of your life.

That leaves us about ten years of free time on our hands, where we can decide what to do, how to do it and how to reap the rewards. Most of us, if we're lucky enough to have a mom and dad, spend the first two decades of our lives under someone else's roof, where we live by their (Mom and Dad's) rules. We can't wait to go out on our own so we can decide for ourselves what we will do with our lives.

What most people decide to do, men and women alike, is to get married. If you take a sane look at this phenomenon, men and women go from living in their parents' household and living by their rules directly into another household, where they live by someone else's rules and have to account for what they do, who they're with and what time they have to be home. And, of course, if the answers aren't satisfactory, you (usually men) will have hell to pay!

Now remember, we have about ten years of actual free time when we can choose for ourselves what to do. I respectfully submit that the scenario of living under this "other roof" is more appealing to women than men. But most importantly, by and large, it is enormously more economically beneficial to women than men. More on this to come a little later...*much more*. Because who you live with and marry is one of the most critical decisions you will ever make.

I haven't addressed at all what you want to do with yourselves or what careers you've chosen. This is strictly an overview of the choices you have in life. And I hope you will see that the decisions we make start very early in life.

# Again...

- What are you doing with your time? Time is money!

- If you have a place to live and food to eat, you are "in the game." Where are you going from here?

- Do you understand the basic rules of business: supply and demand, creating and selling a product?

- What are your hobbies and passions? What do you love to do?

- The harder you work, the luckier you will get.

- I suppose the real question is, *do you want more money or less?* Because how you respond to the questions above may be an indication of whether you will *get* more money...or less.

# CHAPTER THREE

# In the Game

After I graduated from high school I entered Sullivan County Community College, part of the New York state university system. While I was attending the first two years of college, on the weekends and sometimes in the afternoons, I was a lifeguard at the Pines Hotel. In the summers, I worked at a food and equipment warehouse called Zakarin Brothers, plus I had my college rock-and-roll band. For all intents and purposes, I was totally self-sufficient. I had taken out a bank loan to pay for my education. I also had at least two jobs, and between them I made in the neighborhood of $300 a week, sometimes more.

On weekends during the school year most of the guys stayed in their dorm rooms and watched sports. I set up shop in my room and started a small cottage industry: typing term papers for fifty cents a page. I had taken typing and dictation classes in high school (in case you're wondering why, here's a big hint: I was the only guy in the class) and had become a very adept typist. I was very fast, about ninety words a minute, so typing one double-spaced page took just a few minutes. All the guys in the dorm wanted their term papers to look as good as mine, so they would hand me their scratched-out handwritten papers to retype or simply stand over my shoulder and dictate as I typed. I could finish off a term paper in no time at all, which of course resulted in more cash. A thirty-page, double-spaced paper took me less than an hour to complete. I earned $15.

The band I played in in Upstate New York (and I hesitate to say this) was called Bullfrog Bheer. The "h" was put in for effect.

I'm afraid I came up with the name. Though the other band members were more talented musicians than I was, in short order they were playing songs I had written, even though I could barely play guitar (there was already a bass player in the band). I was relegated to sometimes singing lead, sometimes strumming along on guitar. It wasn't my band—I had joined an already existing band—but by virtue of the fact they were playing my songs it became my band.

Again, more popularity, more girls, and more money—my three favorite things.

By the time I graduated from Sullivan County Community College and got my Associate degree, I had amassed close to $10,000. I moved back in with my mother when I returned to New York City to attend Richmond College in Staten Island, part of the New York City University system, for the last two years of my college education. Though it wasn't cool to be living with Mom at age nineteen, I was happy to do so. I saved rent and food money, plus I didn't have to buy furniture or pay electric and water bills. Whatever money I earned, I got to keep.

> Though it wasn't **cool** to be living with mom at age nineteen, I was happy to do so. I saved rent and food money, plus I didn't have to buy furniture or pay electric and water bills. Whatever money I earned, **I got to keep.**

I went to a music store and bought the best state of the art equipment of the day: Marshall guitar amplifiers. I bought them secondhand. I bought a Marshall 100-watt RMS amplifier and a Marshall 200-watt RMS amplifier with the speakers. Together they cost three or four thousand dollars. They were and continue to be

Here is a list of the songs I had written by 1971. I felt confident they could land me a solo record. Solo artists, it occurred to me, got to keep the lion's share of monies. They didn't have to split the earnings with anyone else. And if I wrote my own songs and sang them, I could always hire musicians to round out my band. They would be "work for hire."

The above flies in the face of the fantasy-filled notions most people have about bands and about music in general. They believe it just "happens." No one seems to know why bands break up so quickly, or why they turn on each other after they break up when (while they were together) everything was peachy-keen. Everyone has this notion that musicians just sort of bump into each other and form bands. No one puts much thought into the inner workings and dynamics of a band, which is why "after the fact" (when bands disband) they sue each other—similar to marriage. No one discusses a "sunset clause," and no one discusses the "cost" of marriage.

I was aware the industry I was getting into was called the MUSIC BUSINESS. It's an interesting phrase, really. Because it combines the creative (music) with the pragmatic (business). But if one understands that the only thing we can fairly expect from life is full disclosure before the fact, how can anyone complain they didn't know? And the law says ignorance is no excuse. It says right there in bold headlines, the MUSIC BUSINESS—music and the business (of music).

I started thinking. If I started a band, who decides which song is going to make the grade? Who can be fired and who can't? Who owns the name of the band? If everyone within the band isn't working as hard, should the band split the monies evenly? If the lead singer is why everyone comes to see the band, should he get more? All these questions and more were what I thought about.

I could always form a band. But why not try to go it alone? If I failed, I always had a fallback position.

In the beginning, before I actually ran into the wall of reality, and partly because of my inexperience, I thought I was much better than I actually was. Good for my self-esteem. Bad for being realistic. In some ways, it's a quality I still possess. I always go for it, even though the chances for success are small. Since failure to reach for the stars doesn't seem to have many consequences, why not go for it?

ORIGINAL
→ DOOT-DOOT SONG
→ SHE KNOWS
→ THE AMEN CORNER
— MOON MAIDEN
→ STANLey THE PARROT

LITTLE lady
WHEN I AWOKE

→ FEEL LAZY
I AMR A NEW MAN

ESKIMO SUN (a 6-Month Waltz)

(I think) I'M GOING DOWN (anymore)

I REARRANGE

→ THE SIMPLE TYPE

MUSIC BUSINESS

the best amplifiers made; they are the same amplifiers professional bands use. On occasion, when I was between bands, I would rent the amplifiers out to other bands.

While I was in Richmond College, my priorities shifted. I switched from a journalism major (I had delusions of becoming a newspaper reporter) to focusing on getting a Bachelor of Arts degree in education. I figured I could always find a teaching job. It was a profession that, while not high-paying, was always in demand. Plus the working hours were short, leaving me plenty of time to do other things I enjoyed more. These were my thoughts at the time.

So, here I was, living with Mom and trying to finish my college education. In the afternoons after classes I worked at odd jobs, such as in a deli, where I was paid pocket change as well as all I could eat. I had my band, which picked up more loose change.

My childhood love of comic books hadn't diminished; in fact it continues to this day. Because I knew quite a lot about comic books, I understood their value. If this sounds strange to you, think of all the people who have attics full of bric-a-brac and potpourri gathering dust. They don't have a clue what the value of their stuff is and get rid of it for pennies on the dollar at flea markets. I knew people had attics full of comic books from their youth, and that some of those old comics were true collectors' items. Using the mimeograph machine my mother had bought me, I created a flyer saying I was interested in buying comic books for a dollar a pound. People thought that instead of throwing out their old comic books, if they could get $100 for a hundred pounds of their old stuff it would be worth it.

I didn't think anyone wanted to hear my life story on my flyer. Also, I had to grab everyone's attention. The best way to do that was to make sure that the first word was the most important word. CASH, CASH PAID FOR COMIC BOOKS—and then my telephone number. I printed a few hundred flyers. When I took the subway to college each day I left flyers on the subway seats. The subway

October 17 1972

Mr. Gene Klein
155-07 59th Avenue
Flushing NY  11355

    As President of Local 802, it is with great pleasure that I welcome you as a member of our Local.

    The strength of our Union depends on the cooperation of the most important person, you the member. Your ideas and suggestions will always be welcome.

    Please feel free to call on me at any time for whatever assistance you might need.

Fraternally yours,

MLA:pfs

MAX L. ARONS, President
Local 802, A.F.M.

*Patronize Live Music*

---

> In 1972, I was finishing my college studies and my first band, Wicked Lester, was starting to get off the ground. Before our proposed record for Epic could be released, and before we could be paid for having played on our own record, we had to join the musicians union. When I finally received the notification that I had been accepted (after I sent in my $35 dues), I felt elated. I was legitimate. I was a professional musician.
>     And I was still living at my mother's house.

was my delivery system—it went all over the city of New York. People riding the train would see the flyer, and some might write down the phone number. The subway carried my message...*for free.*

I had learned the value of comic books by going into comic book stores and seeing the prices posted. I went to these stores not only as a fan and buyer of comic books, but also to learn about their value. Now even though the dealer was willing to sell you Action Comics #1 for $35,000, if I actually walked in with an Action Comics #1 and tried to sell it to him, after much back-and-forth we would eventually settle on the price he would pay me, which was about half. The dealer would then turn around and charge the customer twice as much.

A pound equals about twenty comic books; a hundred pounds is an awful lot of comic books. For $100, my chances were very good that somewhere in that pile there would be nuggets of gold. I averaged about 10 percent—that is, about one in ten comic books in the pile turned out to be worth tens, hundreds, sometimes even thousands of dollars. I knew when people in their fifties got rid of their comic book collections I was hitting a gold mine. They were unaware of the comics' value, and the older they were, the better chance I had of getting a thousand-dollar comic book. In a very real way, comic books paid for my college education. Had I been seriously interested in that field I could certainly have continued and succeeded in the comic book field and dealing in collectibles. I could have opened up my own comic book store. But I had other dreams.

One of my schoolmates decided to attend economics school. He felt his future lay on Wall Street—that it was a place with no limits. He was probably right. It's the place of dreams, it's a place where you can make enormous amounts of money. But the interesting thing was that while he was going to school studying economics, on weekends, almost without fail, he would go to flea markets. He loved bric-a-brac, potpourri and other silly, childish-sounding words that usually mean nothing more than you're buy-ing and selling garbage. He loved buying and selling garbage. He was not a Disney fan. He didn't collect Barbie dolls or antiques. He just liked to go to flea markets. He loved the social environment. He was a flea market junkie.

He went on to graduate from his school of economics and get a job on Wall Street. In short order, he became quite successful. Within two years he was earning over $100,000 a year. His lifestyle improved, and still every weekend he went to flea markets. Once or twice I accompanied him but would eventually have to leave him there. He would stay from sunup to sundown. He would have his lunch there, he sipped coffee there; he just loved the atmos-phere. As it turned out, although he was making a lot of money on Wall Street, he wasn't enjoying it. He made no money at flea mar-kets, but he loved them.

Let's skip a few pages and get to the point. He's now one of the top two or three flea market people in the New York-New Jersey-Philadelphia tristate area. If you go to a flea market, chances are you're going to one of his. He lives, breathes and eats flea markets. And he does it better because he loves it. He works longer hours than he ever would on Wall Street; he doesn't have any "social security"—that is, no one pays him an actual weekly salary, so it's a much riskier way to earn a living. But he is a multi-millionaire many times over. He's gone on to buy multiacre properties in the heart of several cities. He now actually owns the land he holds the flea markets on. When he doesn't have flea markets going, he rents the space out to industrial and parking concerns. He's no longer just a flea-market mogul; he's now in the real estate business and the parking business. And Wall Street? A lot of those guys work for him now, investing his money.

You can do this too! Figuratively speaking, there's nothing pre-venting you from becoming a flea-market mogul at the same time you're planning to become a Wall Street trader. So many people literally have a gold mine they're sitting on and don't realize it. We all do things in our spare time we love passionately that can, in fact, make us more money than the jobs we work at, whether it's watching football games or going to flea markets.

Say you go to dental school; you want to become a dentist because it pays well. While you're going to dental school (which is going to take you ten or twelve years, after which you can earn $70,000 to $150,000 a year or more) you notice that you're actually better at picking out fabric for materials than your wife or girlfriend is. If you're planning to be a dentist and you're more interested in Persian carpets, I'm here to caution you that you might wind up being a carpet salesman. When you really think about it, a dentist is much more important to the planet we all share than a carpet salesman. If carpet salesmen ceased to exist, nothing would be affected, but if dentists ceased to exist, we would be walking around with a mouthful of pain.

A visit to the dentist, even a complete overhaul of your teeth including periodontal surgery, might set you back five grand. A good Persian carpet will cost you multiple times that. A dentist's overhead includes expensive equipment. Going to medical school is not only expensive, it is time-consuming when you look at the amount of money you might have earned had you been working. The prerequisite for becoming a carpet salesman is minimal. You don't need to buy equipment; you don't need to train or pass exams. All you need to do is have "people skills." The carpet

> So many people literally have a **gold mine** they're sitting on and don't realize it. We all do things in our spare time we love passionately that can, in fact, **make us more money** than the jobs we work at.

salesman might make more money than the dentist. The rock star will make more money than the teacher. If you try one or two non-essential pursuits—let's call them "hobbies"—at the same time you are preparing to "work" for a living, you never know if any of these will actually become your pot of gold at the end of the rainbow.

We all know more about our hobbies than our jobs. We also love our hobbies more than our jobs. Figure out a way to make money off your hobbies (but hold on to your job). Mrs. Fields was an attractive young housewife (twenty years old) who wanted to do more with her life. As the legend goes, she had no working experience and very little knowledge of the world of business. She *did* know how to bake a mean cookie. She couldn't qualify for a bank loan; even her husband told her she would never make any money. (He eventually wound up working for her.) Mrs. Fields Cookies...maybe you've heard of it. She's taken a lot of my money; I'm sure she's taken some of yours. She did what she loved doing. You can too. But again, don't ever only do one thing. Always do multiple things. We all love many things in our lives. One or more of them may actually make us more money than the jobs we hate to work at.

> If the day ever comes and you're lucky enough to make enough money from your hobby, do it full-time. You will be blessed to be working at something you love.
>
> Like my friend. Like me.

If the day ever comes and you're lucky enough to make enough money from your hobby, do it full-time. You will be blessed to be working at something you love.

Like my friend. Like me.

So figure out what it is you love to do (that should be easy), but be *realistic*. What does realistic actually mean? Well, it means that if you want to become a sumo wrestler and you stand five-feet tall and weigh ninety-eight pounds (whether you're a man or a woman) I would strongly urge you not to get involved in that field. It also happens not to be a very high-paying job. Sumo wrestlers are popular in Japan; the rest of the world couldn't care less. There's minimal or nonexistent licensing/merchandising potential.

American sports pay more money than almost any job on the face of the planet, but again, your chances of becoming successful in American sports are slim. For every basketball player who earns $20 million a year, there are millions of corpses along the roadside. So on the weekends play your basketball games, but during the week have a job. And have another hobby or passion at the same time. Also, measure your height. If you're approaching seven feet, keep that option open. If you're approaching six feet, forget it. And yes, I know, you're a better basketball player than anyone else where you live, in Sandusky, Ohio. But I'm still telling you to forget it.

For those of you who don't think money is everything, try this one on for size: I know a man who gave up sex and rich food. He was healthy right up until the day he killed himself. Try to be realistic about life. You may not become the richest person who ever lived. But there's always a chance of becoming richer than you are now. Certainly you have a very good chance of not being poor.

 ***I don't know anything about music, but in my line you don't have to.*** —ELVIS PRESLEY

He was right, of course. The main point about putting in Elvis's comment is that education, qualification and all the other big words may not actually have very much to do with succeeding and acquiring wealth at all. It is possible to devote your entire life to deep political thinking and never wind up being the president of the United States; or you can be a very bad B-movie actor and scale the heights to become the president of the United States.

Either way, stay out of politics—it's a waste of time, financially anyway. It is a nice place to get your name up in lights, but in order to reap any financial benefits, you have to wait until you're out of office to write books, go on lecture tours, make big money. You also have to go to school for many more years than I would suggest. Politics historically has been a rich man's game, and actually is a loss-leader. Forget it. If your ultimate goal is to acquire riches, don't ever run for public office. They don't get paid well. The president gets paid around $400,000 a year. After taxes, that's about $200,000.

Because America is the great free society, perhaps the most open society that has ever existed on the face of this planet, it has unlimited entrepreneurial opportunities. You can get rich. Certainly have more money than you have now. And be realistic and honest with yourself. Wanting riches is good.

A very important point that isn't taught in business school: America, which the rest of the world calls a land without culture, ironically invented the culture that is worshiped around the world. Hamburgers are universal. Rock-and-roll is universal. American movies are universal. Jeans are universal. The American culture is universal. The interesting thing about this American culture, this so-called "culture of pop," is that it has no history. Kings and queens had nothing to say about it. This culture was created by the lowest dregs of society, the poorest and often the blackest. American music—blues, jazz and rock-and-roll—were created by the sons of black slaves. It is a primitive form of music. You don't have to go to music school to understand how to play it; you just have to feel it. It is instantly accessible around the world. Japanese music, however, is not. Outside of Japan, and I mean this in the nicest way with all due respect, nobody cares about Japanese music. And that goes for balalaika music and Australian Aboriginal music too. Nobody cares. The whole world loves American culture, and because of that you have many opportunities that could be financially beneficial.

What I do, which is play in a rock band, is part of this "American culture" the world is willing to pay lots of money for. It's American music, television, movies, food and clothing (jeans, etc.) You may want to consider entering one or more of these areas—as a hobby or as a job. Remember, the limit is the world. If you're not original, copy!! But copy stuff people will buy. Wanna go into "foods"? Stay away from frogs' legs. People won't put webbed feet into their mouths. This ain't France. We like burgers. So does the rest of the world. Got it?

*     *     *

With my hobby, music, I instinctively knew that the next step was going into a recording studio and seeing what the songs I had written sounded like. The first two songs I wrote were called "Leeta," which had Beatles overtones, and "My Uncle is a Raft," which sounded like a Nitty Gritty Dirt Band tune. Incidentally, for those of you who are curious about "Leeta," it was included in the KISS Boxed Set that was released in 2002...and earned gold status.

I started writing more songs and decided to demo them up ("demo" is short for demonstration tape). Brooke Ostrander, who taught music in a public school, also had recording equipment and played keyboards. He helped me put together a demo tape of my songs, which I took and dutifully went knocking on record company doors, trying to get a recording contract as a solo artist. In those days my name was Gene Klein (because Klein was my mother's maiden name). No one bit—I didn't get a solo recording contract.

I thought the next step might be to put a band together, to show people that these songs actually worked live, and that a band was viable. I got in touch with my old school chum Stephen Coronel who had played with me in several bands, including The Long Island Sounds, and with whom I'd written a few songs. We eventually got a band together consisting of five people, including a rhythm guitarist named Stanley Eisen, who would later become Paul Stanley, my partner for over thirty years. The new band was called Wicked Lester.

Our maiden voyage was a gig for $125 playing at the Richmond College Armory. We didn't make a lot of money, but we were playing original songs—Paul's and mine. The second show we played was in New Jersey, at a B'nai B'rith youth conference for parents and their thirteen-year-old girls. We made another $150 or so, though some of that money was taken up renting a truck. Along the way there were a few other gigs, some more doors got opened and eventually we got a recording contract with Epic Records. We recorded an album, produced by Ron Johnsen, at Electric Lady Studios. The album was completed and the label seemed happy enough, and ostensibly I had gotten what I wanted. But Paul and I looked at each other and believed then, as we do now, that the band didn't have what it took to go the distance. A single wasn't enough for us. Nothing but a home run would do.

Epic Records told us Wicked Lester was fine and that they were happy with the album, but Stephen Coronel, our guitar player and my old school buddy, had to go! I was given the unpleasant task of informing him of this news. Before I went to see him, and even though my heart was breaking, I sat down and typed up a letter of understanding, saying in essence that for $200 Stephen agreed to leave the band, that $200 was his payment in full for his services, and that Epic Records wanted to continue the band without him. I told Stephen the truth, even though it hurt us both, that the band would unfortunately have to continue without him.

SPEED - 3¾ SIDE I     7½ SIDE II

.notes and other misc.

This is a tape made up of 12 songs. The purpose of this
thing is to show you what I have. I tried to include a
sample of at least every type of thing I do..

As to wants: a contract with a label would be fine, along
with manager/producer (et al), which is why you're getting
this. Oh yes, I'm...

        Gene Klein    353-1235
        155-07 50th Ave.
        Flushing, NY 11355

IMPORTANT NOTE - as to Speed: find out for yourself (could
be either 7½ or 3¾). Re TAPE CONTROLS: take off all bass
responses on your tape recorder with a little treble for
finest results.

Re the material: all the material is composed by me, with
the exception of About Her and Little Lady which were composed in collaboration. Drums were excluded for reasons
having to do with the clarity of the tape.
        The material then, is...

| | | |
|---|---|---|
| Little Lady (Coronel-Klein) | | 3:25 |
| Put On Your Slippers (Klein) | | 2:40 |
| About Her (Coronel-Klein) | | 5:30 |
| Amen Corner (Klein) | | 1:55 |
| Feel Lazy Today (Klein) | | 2:35 |
| A Reevus In The Eye -nancy- (Klein) | | 1:25 |
| Leeta (Klein) | | 2:15 |
| Moon Maiden (Klein) | | 3:35 |
| Eskimo Sun (Klein) | | 3:55 |
| When I Awoke (Klein) | | 4:15 |
| A Story (Klein) | | 2:10 |
| Stanley The Parrot (Klein) | | 6:10 |

PROBABLY - ALL MATERIAL ON ONE SIDE
~~Note: You'll have to eventually turn the tape over to hear
all the stuff. When you get reasonably close to the end
(and you hear nothing) it's time for you to turn it over.~~

*Gene*

*Thank you but - I'll have to*

*Pass*

*Peace*

Wicked Lester had a recording contract with Epic Records. That record with its five members was a hodge-podge of musical styles that sounded like a cross between the Doobie Brothers and Three Dog Night. It tried to cater to a wide range of tastes. While Paul and I were thrilled to have made a record like that, and to have actually gotten a recording contract with a professional record company, wisely or unwisely we decided it wasn't what we wanted to do. We threw caution to the wind and did what we believed in.

Now, to pause for a moment, this sounds like something I don't recommend. A bird in the hand is worth two in the bush. Wicked Lester had a recording contract with Epic Records. Why gamble? Why throw that away? My next band might turn out to be nothing. I felt comfortable taking the risk because I had already amassed

---

*If at first you don't succeed, try and try again.*

This is a note I included with my first demo (demonstration tape) of my original songs. I recorded the material on a home tape recorder at Brooke Ostrander's house. Ostrander was a music teacher in a New Jersey public school. He agreed to let me come over on weekends to record my songs on his recording equipment. He also helped by playing keyboards.

My plan was to have a tape, go around to all the record labels, get a recording contract and only then put a band together. The logic behind this approach was simple pragmatism. To wit: If I first formed a band, and then got a recording contract, the members of the band might think that they would all be entitled to an equal split of the monies. However, if I was able to get a recording contract on my own (a Gene Simmons record contract), then I could go and hire anyone I wanted to play on the record and/or in the band as sidemen, or salaried employees, not partners.

The idea made financial sense. It just didn't work. My material wasn't good enough.

"Little Lady" would become "Goin' Blind" within two years and be recorded by KISS, the band I was yet to start with Paul Stanley. One other song would become the basis for a KISS classic: "Stanley The Parrot" was the initial inspiration behind "Strutter," which Paul took and fashioned into a complete song.

The rest of the songs have yet to see the light of day. Maybe one day.

Notice the "Pass" at the bottom of the page. A pass means "thank you, but no thank you." When I initially heard the term, I thought I had made it. I associated "pass" with "passing a grade"...as in, "Wow. I passed."

After a few passes, I changed my plans and decided to either join a band that could play my songs, or start one.

While all this was going on, I was going to Richmond College, part of the New York City university system, finishing my Bachelor's degree in education. I had plans to become a teacher. If I didn't become a rock star and make tons of money, I could still get up on stage in front of school kids and at least make a living.

Needless to say, I failed as a solo artist. But I did succeed in a band.

a decent amount of money. I could make decisions not from a position of urgency, but purely from a position of strength. I wanted to reach for the stars; it wasn't enough just to reach high. It wasn't enough just to have a career; I wanted to have a huge career. If I was going to lose everything, I had a fallback position. I could work for a living as a teacher.

Paul and I decided to re-form the band—in essence, get rid of everybody else and walk out of our recording contract. If we couldn't have the band our way, we both agreed it simply wasn't worth doing. When Paul and I informed the two remaining members of Wicked Lester that we intended to replace them, they stated that they planned to adhere to the contract and stay in the band. They could not be thrown out. So Paul and I decided to quit the band, knowing full well that Epic Records would not continue Wicked Lester without the two main songwriting members.

Paul Stanley and I wanted to create the band of our dreams, the band we never saw on stage. The band that would combine everything we loved: rock-and-roll, comic books, horror movies...KISS. It was a daring move; I'm not sure if I had it to do over I would make the same decision. But it was clearly the right choice.

When we formed our new band we didn't have the two other members of the band, and we didn't quite know where we were going.

> I wanted to **reach for the stars**; it wasn't enough just to reach high. It wasn't enough just to have a career; I wanted to have a **huge** career. If I was going to lose everything, I had a fallback position. I could work for a living as a teacher.

But we knew we wanted to get there, and fast. In short order, we got a new drummer named Peter Criscoula, whose name we later changed to Peter Criss, and we had a trio. Peter could sing in a very R&B style but was not a schooled musician. He had a volatile temper; he was not well educated and was given to emotional outbursts, but he had charisma. Being young, we tended to be blind to any of those other considerations. We had a trio, and that was all that mattered.

**Paul Stanley and I wanted to create the band of our dreams, the band we never saw on stage. The band that would combine everything we loved: rock-and-roll, comic books, horror movies...KISS.**

Soon we put ads in newspapers and eventually chose Ace Frehley as our lead guitarist. Ace also had some self-esteem issues and was not particularly well-educated; he was apt to give in to the bottle. You don't need a lot of qualifications to be in a rock band. All of this sounds like a volatile mixture, and the truth is, in most cases, it's only a matter of time before it explodes. But that's another story for another time.

A team, whether it's a football team or a financial team, is only as good as the members comprising that team, in the same way that a table is only as solid as the legs holding it up. Needless to say, rock bands aren't the most conservative bet in terms of financial reward. Statistically, the chances of becoming a famous rock star and making money (not necessarily the same thing) are slim to none.

If I was ever going to give it a shot, my early twenties was the right time. The chances of becoming a rock star in your sixties are nil. If you're going to gamble, gamble when you're twenty years old.

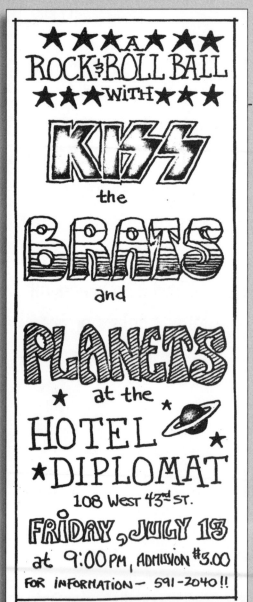

By July of 1973, we had become seasoned veterans, we thought. We had played at an Amityville, Long Island club called the Daisy a few times. We played a club called Coventry in Queens a few times. We even played a "loft party"—the bill was The Brats, Wayne County and the Toilet Boys and us. People were starting to talk about a new band called KISS.

I put together a press kit in the offices of the Puerto Rican Interagency Council after hours. I had full access to photocopy machines, typewriters and office equipment. I bought the year-end issues of the music trade journals: Cashbox, Record World and Billboard. They listed every record company, every manager and every music lawyer. Paul helped me write our bio. Peter's friend in the printing business printed up our press kit, and I sent out the mailing to record companies, producers and managers.

Our debut to a midtown New York City crowd came at the Diplomat Hotel ballroom. Paul and I rented the place. The Brats were paid $350 to headline, since they were a local draw. We would go on second. We paid the Planets $150. Notice KISS is headlining in the newspaper ad Ace drew.

Since we were the "promoters" of the concert, for an admission price of $5, multiplied by an audience of 500, we grossed $2,500. We had to pay the rental fee of about $1,200. We also paid the other bands. Even though we were not the headliners, the music business, or more accurately, the business of music, was starting to become very clear to me. As headliners the Brats would get $350, and even though we were opening for them, we would net out (after expenses) about $750—more than twice the amount they received.

But the risk of failure (and incurring all the expense) was relegated to Paul and me. Ace and Peter either didn't have money or refused to take the risk.

If you're going to fail, better to fail when you're twenty than when you're sixty.

People think the prerequisite to being in a rock band is a thorough musical education. Here's a shocker: almost all the popular musicians and singers whose CDs you love and buy on a regular basis are probably not only completely oblivious to the notions of music theory, having never gone to music school, but they most likely can't read or write musical notations either. They simply play or sing by ear. And none of the foregoing, of course, counts the successful artists who also happen to be tone deaf.

> If you're going to **gamble**, gamble when you're twenty years old. If you're going to **fail**, better to fail when you're twenty than when you're sixty.

The appeal of becoming a rock star wasn't simply the access to the female population of the world (and I'm told there are more females than males). It was also the chance to earn more money than God. *That* was a risk worth taking. I'm here to tell you that the true appeal of being a rock star is (get ready for it) girls and money—lots of both. Again, any rock star that tells you otherwise is lying!

But as part of KISS I also had to deal with two other guys who could barely hold down a job (if they worked at all!) None of this is meant to sound mean-spirited to either Ace or Peter. I cared for them then; I care for them now. But these are the facts: Peter Criss was being supported by his wife (he got married before he got famous. It was only a matter of time before he had to pay her an enormous sum when they divorced. I'll cut to the chase here: Peter had two more marriages to come; he also had to pay wife number two enormous sums. There were three wives in all.). In matters of

> I'm here to tell you that the true appeal of being a rock star is (get ready for it) **girls and money—** lots of both. Again, any rock star that tells you otherwise is **lying!**

the heart, perhaps, Peter decided rightfully for himself; in matters of the pocketbook, in my opinion, he couldn't have made worse decisions.

In 1972 Ace Frehley was working part time as a "liquor delivery boy." That job soon dissolved and Ace was left penniless. Paul, my sober partner and brother-in-arms, was the one I often turned to for support, opinions and advice.

Bands need amplifiers and equipment and guitars. They need rehearsal space and rent money and trucks to carry equipment back and forth. All this costs a lot of money. Peter and Ace barely had enough to take the subway home from rehearsal. They often asked me to loan them twenty-five cents for the subway ride home, or to lend them enough to buy a hot dog. Rent was hardly ever shared by all four; I usually wound up paying the lion's share. Paul and I bought all the equipment; Ace and Peter shared none of the costs. When it was time to sign a management contract with our first manager, no one could afford to pay the lawyer. I fronted the band the full cost. I also lent our manager enough money to pay *his* lawyer, because he couldn't afford to pay one either. In hindsight, it was probably a conflict of interest in legal terms. But it was necessary.

At that time I was working at the Puerto Rican Interagency Council as the assistant to the director. As such, I was paid well. I opened the offices and closed them daily and pretty much had the run of the place. When the office was empty I would avail myself (and the band) of the photocopying machines, the typewriters and all of the other office equipment so I could put our press kit together. I also

BRASS RING PRODUCTIONS PRESENTS

# "the OUTRAGEOUS"

# KISS

## Also Special Guest
With Flint's "SMACK DAB" MIKE QUATRO JAM BAND

# FRI. APRIL 4, 8:00 PM
# NORDIC ARENA, M-59 AT US-23

*Tickets $4.50 Advance, $5.50 Day of Show*

*Flint - Boogie Records, Miller Road
    Record Land, Eastland Mall*
*Howell - Schaffer's House of Music
    (on Grand River)*
*Saginaw - Merry-Go-Round*

*Grand Blanc - Proffer's Sound Center,
    Beula Vista Mall*
*Brighton - Schaffer's House of Music*

*Pontiac - Hudson's Pontiac Mall*

*ALSO AVAILABLE AT NORDIC ARENA, BOX OFFICE, HARTLAND, MICHIGAN*

---

*A concert flyer advertising KISS with opening band, the Mike Quatro Jam Band. The irony of this bill is that our very first shows (even before our first album was released) were in Canada. We were filling in for missed dates by the Quatro Band. And a few months later, here we were headlining over them. Quatro, incidentally, is the brother of Suzi Quatro, who was a female rocker in the 70s.*

sent out our mailings. I picked up the phone and made calls to local clubs, trying to entice them into giving a brand-new band called KISS a shot. Nobody wanted to book a band that didn't play the hits of the day. We were an all-original band who wore more make-up and higher heels than most people's mothers, so initially it wasn't an easy sell.

When KISS recorded its debut album in 1973 at Bell Sound Studios in New York City, Bill Aucoin, our first manager, put each of us on a $75-a-week salary. I had finished college and for a time I sublet an apartment. As soon as I saw the specter of going out on tour with KISS, I found the idea of paying rent on an apartment I wouldn't be in the height of stupidity. So I moved back in with my mother once again, this time at age twenty-four, and cut back all my costs. I'd be out on tour most of the year, anyway! For the most part, I used my $75 a week for spending money.

Paul likewise was living at home. Peter was living in a house that his working wife paid for. KISS became successful very fast, but real money didn't come in for at least another couple of years, and we were always playing catch-up.

We were deeply in the hole on our first tour, funded by Bill Aucoin's overdrawn American Express card. We shared hotel rooms and ate for free at the afternoon concert hall meals provided for the crew. But I had no other financial exposure (no marriage or children, no girlfriend—just "friends"—no car payments, no mortgages, no phone bills, and I hardly ever bought clothes). I was fine. I was surviving. I was in the game. There was nowhere to go but up.

> **Nobody wanted to book a band that didn't play the hits of the day. We were an all-original band who wore more make-up and higher heels than most people's mothers, so initially it wasn't an easy sell.**

# Again...

- Do you want to be your own boss or work for someone else?

- Do you want the material things now, or can you wait to get them all later?

- Can you make money from your hobby and amass riches doing what you love? What is your potential goldmine?

- What is your dream? Go for it...while you're young! Gamble when you're twenty years old!

- On the other hand, what is your fallback position? What's the backup plan if your dream doesn't come true?

- *Are you minimizing your financial exposure and maximizing your earning potential?*

## What I mean is:

- Are you a male, twenty years old, and about to marry? DON'T! (not now, not ever!)

- Are you working overtime, as much as you can get? GOOD!

- Do you have a hobby you're passionate about besides your job? GOOD (but don't spend too much money on your hobbies).

# CHAPTER FOUR

# My Life with KISS

**W**ithin a year and a half of releasing our debut album (*KISS*, February '74), KISS was playing Anaheim Stadium in California to a sold-out crowd of about 60,000 people. Bands didn't usually play stadiums then. The Beatles had. Our opening acts were bands that had been around for at least a decade before KISS: Bob Seger, Ted Nugent, Uriah Heep. We were an upstart. We were at the beginning of a rise that would last decades.

At the time of this first big tsunami of success in the mid-seventies my personal exposure (the amount of money I had to pay out every month) was $200 for a co-op I was subletting in New York City. I didn't drive and had never owned a car, so I had no car payments, no gas, no insurance, no nothing. I also obviously never had a wreck, or the costs that come with it. I hardly ever went shopping for clothing, because I had leather pants and a T-shirt. I had no steady girlfriends to support, though I had plenty of liaisons—usually indoors, devoid of the costs of movies, dinners and wasted time.

Living in Manhattan or any large city affords you the opportunity of taking cabs or the bus without worrying if your car will be there the next day. Also, in a cab a "chauffeur" drives you. The very first car I ever bought was at the age of thirty-five—and I bought it secondhand. Until that time I didn't even know how to drive. I had never taken a vacation, but I had a ball doing everything I wanted to do, working seven days a week. I have yet to take a real vacation, and I'm fifty-three. Every day of my life is a vaca-

# The AGORA presents

### 'IN CONCERT

## KISS

### WITH SPECIAL SURPRISE GUESTS

## *Games!... Pagent!... Fun!...*

## For The Wednesday October 30th
## HALLOWEEN PARTY

Doors Open     7:30p.m.
Show Starts     9:00p.m.

## TICKETS ONLY AVAILABLE
## AT THE DOOR

$3.00    non-dressed
$2.00    costume dressed

### PROOF OF AGE 18 AND OVER REQUIRED

*This is a flyer that was sent out for a club show in Ohio during our first tour in 1974. We had yet to have control of our concert poster advertising, so often the posters looked like those you would see for a high school dance. Also during this period we were on tour opening for Manfred Mann and Savoy Brown, two English bands. When the tour wasn't playing a date, we played fill-in dates, like this one at the Agora.*

tion, because it's my choice to do what I want to do and when I want to do it!

The idea that anybody in their twenties or thirties would ever think about taking a vacation before they've amassed fame and fortune is a wonderful idea—*for losers*. Not everyone can climb Mount Olympus; somebody's got to wrap fish. Perhaps it's Nature's way of weeding out the winners from the losers. Those who work harder make more money—period. Two people who work at the same job and earn the same salary and have the same relative talent will make the same amount of money if they work the same number of hours per week. However, if one decides to work on the weekends, he or she will not only make more money, but usually at double or triple rates...and of course your boss will take note, hint, hint!

Let's take a look at this notion for a moment. You haven't decided what your career plans are. You're twenty years old and you work a nine-to-five job. So in the evening there's a lot of time for socializing. You can always go to a bar or club and meet lots of boyfriends and girlfriends. During the daytime, unless you're a soap opera fan, there's not much to watch on television. You have the option of working. If you're going to work, you have the option of working five days a week or seven days a week. If you work an extra two days a week—and we're only talking from nine to five, remember—you

> The idea that anybody in their twenties or thirties would ever think about taking a vacation before they've amassed fame and fortune is a wonderful idea—*for losers.* Not everyone can climb Mount Olympus; somebody's got to wrap fish.

will make twice as much money on those two extra days, at the very least —maybe more. Because you will be paid at least double time.

If there are fifty-two weeks in a year, and you're working the weekends as well, you've just worked 104 more days! (52 x 2 = 104). If you make twice as much money in those two days, you are in essence working four more days a week. (Double time pay x 2 = 4 days' pay). Then 104 days at double time is 208 more days of pay. (104 x 2 = 208). Try this at triple time and you get 312 days...multiply *that* by whatever you get paid per day!

Let's run through this again. You work five days a week for fifty-two weeks. But you take two weeks off for vacation, you take off Christmas, Thanksgiving, Labor Day, President's Day, Forgot-to-Wipe-My-Ass-Day...you get the picture. You hardly work! If you worked those two extra days each week (the weekends) you would, in essence, almost double your earning power for the entire year! It also means there's a quantum and qualitative effect. If I was the boss, and I saw your work ethic, you wouldn't have to work a full year for me to realize you were a go-getter. Before the first year was up I would have already promoted you.

Some people are go-getters. In the movie industry they're called movers and shakers. If it's more important to you to stay home on Sundays and watch sports, your girlfriend is going to get bored. She's probably going to start looking for guys like me, who don't watch sports on television. More importantly, you're not going to be making more money, and remember, your girlfriend likes you, but she also likes money.

Always keep in mind that money is the single most important tool that will unlock the keys to all of the doors of your happiness. If you don't take weekends off, and you don't take vacations, you still have seven evenings a week of unlimited time to do whatever you want, every night of the week, anytime after 5P.M. None of the clubs are open during the day. Girls don't put on high heels and make-up until nighttime. Usually, you won't "get lucky" until night falls. So you might as well make money until it does.

And, of course, once you make money, don't spend it— not all of it, anyway. Nature gives us big hints. Ever notice those little squirrels? During the summer months they go around and gather nuts. They also bury their nuts, because in the winter there aren't any. If squirrels know what to do with their nuts, why don't men?

> **Ever notice those little squirrels? During the summer months they go around and gather nuts. They also bury their nuts, because in the winter there aren't any. If squirrels know what to do with their nuts, why don't men?**

\* \* \*

While KISS was on tour, the food was free; that's part of touring. I didn't pay for transportation or hotels—all that was part of the tour cost. So when I made money it was in big chunks, and the only cost I had was taxes. The vast majority of the money I made, I saved.

Around 1976 I started voraciously reading and asking questions. *Billboard, Fortune, Wall Street Journal.* You should too. If you don't know something, ask! Anyone! Everyone! Information is everything, and everybody is willing to tell you what you want to know. Religion may be the opiate of the masses or it may be the single thing that may save mankind from itself; but make no mistake about it, the House of God is the library. *Knowledge is everything,* and the law tells us that ignorance is no excuse for not knowing the law.

Keep your mouth shut. Be a vampire. Suck life dry of its knowledge. Go to libraries. Be around more successful people. Be

> The House of God is the library. *Knowledge is everything,* and the law tells us that ignorance is no excuse for not knowing the law.

around the rich and devour everything they know. Too many people quit looking for work as soon as they find a job. That may take you awhile to digest, but it's really what this book is about. It's never about a job. It is, in fact, always about work. If you work, you'll always get paid. If you have a job, you might lose it.

Hang around smart people—like them. Try to hang around rich people—love them, especially people who were poor and became rich. There's a method to their madness. People who win the lottery don't stay rich. Anybody can lose it in an afternoon. Being rich and staying rich means they know something you don't.

"Love the rich"—it's not what we've been taught. What society teaches us—incorrectly, I might add—is that "The rich are different than you and I." Or perhaps you've heard this one—"The rich aren't as happy as we are." That's a lie. A poor person said that. Not a rich one. Trust me, you'll be happier with more money than with less. If you're going to be a miserable son-of-a-bitch, better to be a *rich*, miserable son-of-a-bitch. Believe me, being rich is better than being poor. If money can't buy happiness, it can at least buy everything else.

> Try to hang around rich people-love them, especially people who were poor and became rich. There's a method to their madness.

There's nothing wrong with being poor that isn't substantially better when you get rich. Put it this way: You may not like rich people, but when was the last time a poor person gave you a job? Hmmmm...again, love the rich.

The other guys started to buy lavishly—particularly Ace and Peter. Multiple cars and multiple houses, and even divorces. The KISS gravy train, however, seemed unstoppable. Money poured in by the millions. By 1977 KISS was the number one Gallup Poll winner, above the Beatles and Led Zeppelin, as the most popular band. This was the first of three years in a row KISS had that distinction!

Our manager Bill Aucoin contacted a gentleman named Ron Boutwell, who had his own merchandising entity. They (Aucoin and Boutwell) entered into a venture to manufacture and distribute most KISS products, from T-shirts to necklaces. It became enormous. Every KISS album contained a small catalog and postage-paid envelope you could stuff your check into and order KISS merchandise.

> You may not like rich people, but when was the last time a poor person gave you a job?

A feat, I'm told, which has never been done before or since by rock bands! The merchandising company became so big that there were entire warehouses in California whose main job was to fulfill orders, which kept pouring in by the tens of thousands, night and day. KISS fans were insatiable. They wanted anything and everything that had KISS on it. KISS was everywhere; there were KISS comic books and belt buckles and action figures. KISS was the number one band in licensing, merchandising, record sales and concert sales. The band had become synonymous with America.

Within a short time, however, we contested the notion that our manager was also part of our licensing and merchandising company. We felt that this relationship in some ways crossed the line, and we looked for some legal advice. We were right.

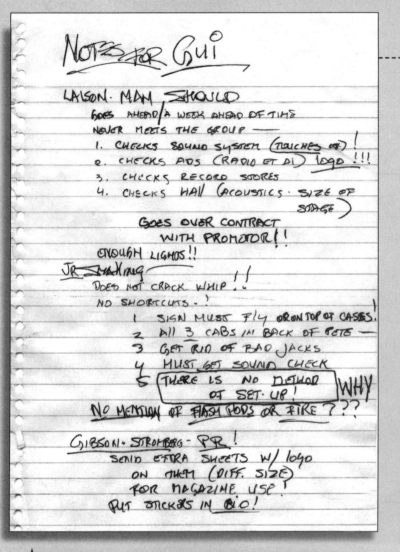

NOTES for Gui

LIAISON· MAN SHOULD
GOES AHEAD/A WEEK AHEAD OF TIME
NEVER MEETS THE GROUP —
1. CHECKS SOUND SYSTEM (TOUCHES OF)
2. CHECKS ADS (RADIO ET AL) logo !!!
3. CHECKS RECORD STORES
4. CHECKS HALL (ACOUSTICS· SIZE OF STAGE)

GOES OVER CONTRACT
WITH PROMOTOR!!
ENOUGH LIGHTS!!
JR MAXING
DOES NOT CRACK WHIP!!
NO SHORTCUTS·
1 SIGN MUST FLY OR ON TOP OF CASES!
2 ALL 3 CABS IN BACK OF PETE —
3 GET RID OF BAD JACKS
4 MUST GET SOUND CHECK
5 THERE IS NO METHOD  WHY
OT SET· UP!
NO MENTION OF FLASH PODS OR FIRE ???

GIBSON + STROMBERG - PR !
SEND EXTRA SHEETS w/ logo
ON THEM (DIFF. SIZE)
FOR MAGAZINE USE!
PUT STICKERS IN BIO!

In 1975, we were just starting to climb the ladder of success. I was a member of the band and was certainly as busy as anyone else performing concerts, doing interviews and so on. For some reason, ever since I can remember, I always seemed to have something to say, not just about the music business but about the business of music.

Clearly I had no experience to have a qualified opinion on how things should run, but I nonetheless would fire off missives to our manager Bill Aucoin and give him an eyeful of what needed to be done, how and by whom. These are "Notes to Gui" (Gui is Bill's French name = Guillame). Our liaison man should (I was sure):

• Check our sound system (make sure it worked).

• Check newspaper advertising to make sure our KISS logo was always used—promoters in those days weren't too savvy and tended to put their ads together without consulting us. The results were often embarrassing.

• Check the local record stores (in the markets we were playing in) to make sure our records were being stocked. If they were not, I thought he should pick up the phone, call our record company, Casablanca Records, and give them all the pertinent info. If he wouldn't do that, who would?

• Check the hall acoustics and the size of the stage—as an opening band we hardly ever had a sound check before we got to go on stage. And, even when we started headlining in those early days, the car drives to the next city were so long, we were barely able to get there in time to put on make-up and hit the stage.

• Go over the contract with the promoter—I wanted to make sure we had enough use of the headliner's light system, and had food available in our dressing room.

• Sign (KISS lighted logo) must fly (be visible in back of the band) or be sitting on top of anvil cases on the floor—some of the shows were late in being set up, and the result was we would hit the stage without our trade-mark lighted KISS logo in back of us. I thought there was no excuse for that. If our road crew didn't have enough time to hoist it up in back of us, they should at least put amplifier cabinets in back of our drummer Peter so it would be visible from the back of the concert hall.

• Must get sound check—We often did not. But if the band couldn't, nothing would prevent the road crew and especially our guitar and drum roadies from picking up our instruments and seeing if they actually worked. They could also check the stage sound level and make sure the guitars didn't feed back.

• There is no method of set-up—Referred to the helter-skelter approach of getting our gear out of the trucks and onto the stage. It was pandemoni-um, complicated by a short set-up period, and mostly impacted by the fact that we were an opening band with nothing to say about anything. At the very least, one thought, you wouldn't put up the drums platform first, in front of the amplifiers, if at the end of the set-up you had to pull the drums in back of the amplifiers. It made more sense to set up the drums off-stage on the ground, put up all the amplifiers first and then, after they were set up, bring up the drums last.

• Our public relations company should send extra sheets with our KISS logo—it seemed to me that if newspaper ads appeared in all different sizes, that the less a promoter had to do with putting our logo on an ad and either enlarging or shrinking it, the more control we had in terms of the "look" of the ad.

• Put stickers (KISS logo) in the bios—This one seemed like a no-brain-er to me, and I wondered why the public relations company didn't give us the idea. After the promoter received his KISS press kit (that told the whole story—the name of the new record, the names of the band members and so on), if he also had a few KISS logo stickers, people could take them and stick 'em where they liked. Our KISS name would then "travel," carrying our message. For free.

These sorts of notes were probably a pain in the butt to our manager, but I didn't really care. I wanted to be in a successful band, and if the other people on the team (support or otherwise) were not doing what I thought needed to be done, I was more than willing to bear the consequences of telling them what they were doing wrong.

I was that kind of a guy then. I am that kind of a guy now.

\*    \*    \*

I started looking to spread out. I saw a band in a Washington, D.C. club called Angel. When the band came offstage, I called Neal Bogart (our record label's president) and urged him to sign the band. He did. I got nothing out of it. But I never knew I should.

I felt a surge of confidence. Maybe I knew something! Maybe I could have a "side business." Then I was invited to see a band called Van Halen at the Starwood Club in Los Angeles. Before their set was over, I ran backstage and waited for the band. I was impressed. They told me they were about to sign with a yogurt manufacturer. I convinced them to let me produce and shop a demo for them.

I flew them to New York, bought David Lee Roth some leather pants and platform shoes, and produced their tape. I signed them to my production company, Man of 1,000 Faces. The tape turned out well, but I couldn't convince the rest of KISS or our manager, Bill Aucoin, that they were the next big thing. I didn't want to stand in Van Halen's way. I decided to tear up the contract and let them go, scot-free. I still believed.

> Believe in your **gut feelings**...your own instincts. Everyone around you will tell you why something won't work. It's up to you to prove them wrong and be there at the finish line to **collect.**

In short order, Van Halen signed with Warner Bros. and became huge. It taught me a lesson. Believe in your gut feelings, your own instincts. Everyone around you will tell you why something won't work. It's up to you to prove them wrong and be there at the finish line to collect.

Failure means nothing. Keep swinging that bat. Sooner or later you'll hit the ball! We've often heard the phrase "Winners are born, not made." It's actually not true. That phrase was written by a loser. It's self-defeating. It means I may as well not even try if I wasn't born a winner, because I'm bound to fail. It's a self-fulfilling prophecy. It's akin to a baseball player afraid to swing the bat because, God forbid, he might miss the ball and get a strike. The truth is you can keep swinging and strike out every time, and keep coming up to bat again. Sooner or later you *will* hit the ball! The word "no" means nothing—another double negative, which is that "yes" means everything.

All you guys out there, it doesn't matter how many girls say "no." It only matters when one girl says "yes." A winner never takes no for an answer. On the days when there's nothing to do, a winner will *find* something to do. On the days when there is no work, a winner will create work. On the day when a winner has won the game, is at the peak of his power and is the actual world record holder, the very next day he will (and should) get up at the crack of dawn and try to break his own record. Life, when you're a winner, is about achieving. More. Not less. A winner never rests on his laurels. A winner only rests when you stick him six feet under.

Contrary to popular belief, winners are not surrounded by other winners. The other winners are too busy trying to win and turn the other winner into a loser. Winners always try to achieve more. Again, the main word here is MORE.

A winner is, in fact, usually surrounded by losers. A winner is fed by losers. A winner is admired by losers. Losers make excuses as to why they aren't winners. A winner who hasn't won will simply try harder the next time. But in his mind, he's always a winner. If he didn't win that race, he's only lost one battle. The war is still to be fought. Never wait for the fat lady to sing.

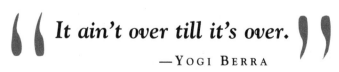

**It ain't over till it's over.**
—YOGI BERRA

*   *   *

By 1979 I still couldn't drive a car and didn't own one. Because of the increase of the amount of money in my life I moved up in the world. I rented the top floor apartment in a building overlooking Central Park for the sum total of $1,500 per month. It had a terrace that overlooked the park. I had yet to buy anything. I was completely flexible and liquid. If I had to move, I would have had no greater damages than a month or two of rent money. I could go anywhere, anytime, without any financial repercussions.

I bought my bed at a Furniture Warehouse. It cost me $250. I splurged only on the things I enjoyed. I had one of the first seven-foot Advent television sets. Other than that, I had no assistants, no maids, no costs other than the bare minimum of being Gene Simmons.

Credit cards, by and large, are for suckers. Pay for your purchases in cash. If you don't have the cash, here's a big hint: *Don't buy it.* You probably don't need it. I know that a fancy car looks awfully good, but take a moment to think it through. You're twenty years old, and you're a guy. The car is hot and you think it will get the girls. You're probably right. The price tag says $40,000. You don't have $40,000. You take out a car loan and let's say you put down 10 percent ($4,000). That leaves 90 percent ($36,000) you have to pay back. Wrong! For lending you the money they're going to make money. Plenty of money. When you're young and have no established credit—or worse, less than perfect credit—they can and will charge you ridiculous interest rates. By the time you're finished paying back that car loan at 10 or 20 percent interest, five years later, that $40,000 car will have cost you somewhere between $50,000 and $60,000. Remember, you're buying that car with after-tax dollars. So, on top of that, add your tax. Unless you're smart enough to know you can deduct interest sometimes!

And don't forget, add to whatever the actual cost of the car is the tax, title, license, gas, insurance, upkeep, and so on. You will probably get laid, because girls do like hot cars. But you must always consider the price. You're better off renting a limo for the night and treating her like a queen than being trapped with a car you're going to have to pay off when you probably don't have the money to do so. Take the bus. Take the subway. And when you want to splurge, rent a car. Don't own cars. Not yet! Don't own houses before you can afford to. Don't get involved in mortgages. Don't take out bank loans. Treat your life as if it was a cash-only proposition. If you don't have the money for something, don't buy it.

> **Treat your life as if it was a cash-only proposition. If you don't have the money for something, don't buy it.**

If you see a house you like that costs $300,000, don't buy it unless you have $300,000 in cash. Because if you have $300,000 saved up, you can put 10 percent down, or 50 percent down, and you'll have money to live on in case you break your leg and can't work for a year. The mortgage payments will still be paid. You must have a buffer against the unforeseen. Because the bank doesn't care that you're a nice person. If you miss a few months, they'll take all the money you've given them, and your house too.

I bought my mother a house, and I did the same for my father. The house I live in now I paid for in cash nineteen years ago. Nineteen years ago the house cost $1.35 million. (I have rebuilt my home since then, and its current value is $15 to $20 million.) I wrote the check and handed it over. No banks, no loans, no misery, no trouble. Free and easy sleep. The accepted wisdom is to take out

a mortgage, but rock-and-roll is risky business, and I wanted to own my own homes (that's plural) without banks breathing down my neck. Never buy anything until you can afford it.

Having said that, almost never pay in cash. Once you have enough money, if something costs $100, and you really want to buy it, figure out a way to put only $10 down and use the money for something else. Try not to pay interest. (Borrow from your family.) Say, I'll give you half this year and half the next year. Hold onto the money. Possession is nine-tenths of the law.

When you get into your car and go on a trip, a long one, most people think, "I'd better have a spare tire," because it's not a matter of *if* I get a flat tire; it's a matter of *when*. That's why cars come equipped with a spare. It's not a matter of being pessimistic or cynical about life. You have to assume the worst, which is that regarding anything you buy, you probably won't have enough money to pay for it and you probably don't need it.

You need to do a spreadsheet, and the numbers have to make sense. You must have a nest egg saved up, just like the squirrel and his nuts. You must have enough saved up in order to take you through the times when nothing's coming in, because there will always be other things you need to buy. Your mother needs an oper ation—some kind of an emergency—it *will* happen. Most people lead their lives foolishly. If they have a dollar they'll spend that dollar.

If you're renting an apartment and paying $900 each month, when you break your leg and can't work, your exposure is minimal. One, two, three months of lost rent money is not so bad. If you can't afford your apartment you'll go to the Motel 6 down the road. And by the way, the beds are just as good. It's all relative; it's all how you look at it. When you sleep, you're completely unaware of your surroundings. The idea is, have enough bread and a quiet place to sleep. The rest is all a figment of our imagination. Keep your money in your pocket. Be cheap like me.

The basic idea, a rule of thumb: You make $500 a week. You're a guy or a girl with a hot date coming up. You see a $500 dress or pair of pants hanging there you really want. Don't buy it. Don't part with $500. Rent it. Buy something else—because (girls) you'll only wear it once.

> **Smart financial planning means always living below your means. Never live at the amount of money you actually earn—never.**

In plain speak, make sure you don't go broke. Smart financial planning means always living below your means. Never live on the amount of money you actually earn—never. Cars, houses—these are all things to buy when you can afford to pay cash for them. Not that you should, mind you!

My philosophy about money, whether I was going to be a teacher or a rock star, was and continues to be the same. Always live at less than half of your means, or even less if you can. Always spend less.

\*     \*     \*

While I was in California planning to record my solo album, making phone calls to various celebrities asking them to appear on it, I came in contact with Cher. We immediately became close friends, then lovers, and soon thereafter moved in together. I moved into *her* Beverly Hills home and lived there, between tours, with Cher and her two children, Chastity and Elijah. Cher had just gotten divorced from Gregg Allman.

I cared for Cher and still do. She was the first girl I had a "relationship" with. I decided to practice what I preached, which was if I were to share my life, whether it would be for a day or a lifetime, the cornerstone of the relationship would be honesty and full disclosure *before* the relationship started, not after. So I told Cher that although I cared for her, I wanted to have a piece of paper between us that defined what our relationship was. We weren't married; I had no plans of ever getting married, and I didn't pretend I did. I wanted to put it in writing.

She never blinked an eye and agreed to the idea that we should both have individual counsel and a piece of paper between us that defined our relationship. It basically said that we were staying together because we wanted to. If and when the day ever came that we split up, what was hers was hers and what was mine was mine. I couldn't ask a dime from her and she couldn't ask a dime from me. There were no joint bank accounts and no joint credit cards.

I noticed when Cher came to visit me in my New York apartment it was not to her liking. She preferred larger living quarters because she had two kids and a nanny. I decided to buy a real showplace. I went shopping with Cher for places that she would like.

We went to the Dakota where John Lennon and Yoko Ono lived, and we were denied, because at that point we were being hounded by the paparazzi. I finally settled on the top floor of what

From left to right: George Klein, my uncle who unfortunately recently passed away, Cher and myself at my mother's house in 1978. My family would get together for Passover dinner, usually at my mother's house. I had started seeing Cher. In a lot of ways, she was my first girlfriend. I grew up never wanting to be tied down; I'm not sure why. So, even though I saw numerous girls socially throughout my life, I never let it become a "relationship." I was too busy being devoted to what I wanted to do, without checking in with someone else first.

And yet when I met Cher, everything changed. Here was someone who had her own career and two children. She was completely self-sufficient. She didn't need me or any man to define who she was. I was drawn to her immediately and wanted to introduce her to my mother.

I will never forget this as long as I live. At the dinner table, Cher's then-two-year-old son Elijah climbed on one of my niece's laps, looked her straight in the eye and spit in her face. Everyone was shocked, and a terrible silence fell over the dinner table. The embarrassment and apologies were eventually dispensed with and dinner continued. But I have to admit when that happened, I wanted to burst out laughing, and, for the entire evening, I had to pinch myself to prevent my laughter from exploding out.

# I KEPT WONDERIN

By 1979, KISS was the number one Gallup Poll winner three years in a row. Above the Beatles. Above Led Zeppelin and the Bee Gees at the height of the disco craze. The media had been trying for years to get photos of the band without our make-up on. Rumors circulated about a $25,000 reward for a photo without our war paint.

The last thing the band and management wanted was to let the cat out of the bag—to give the photographers what they wanted. The more we kept the mystique alive, the better our tickets and merchandise sold. So when I started my relationship with Cher, the band hated it. Management hated it. And the fans hated it. They thought I had lost my edge and the Beast was being domesticated by Beauty. Worst of all, I couldn't even take Cher out to dinner without being descended on by countless paparazzi who were intent on snapping photos of us together and perhaps me, especially, without my KISS make-up on. When we'd go to a restaurant for dinner, it was always done very discreetly. The restaurants were asked and agreed to keep our visit confidential. But by the time we finished eating, the photogs were waiting outside on the sidewalk, in hidden cars (waiting to follow us wherever we went). Restaurant management would come over and tell us the photogs were outside, and I was often forced to take the dinner table napkin and wrap it around my face to hide my identity.

Rumors started to appear in print about supposed facial scars. The press was having a field day trying to figure out why I kept my face hidden. Often when the rumor mags appeared on the stands, completely made-up stories appeared on the cover. And often the photos were "pieced" together.

I never said "I do" in a secret ceremony. Cher never "left her honeymoon bed in tears." There was never a "fistfight over KISS star Gene Simmons" between Cher and Kate Jackson. I DID tell Cher before our relationship began that I'd had many liaisons, but the "1,000 girls" number was incorrect. And my mother never warned Cher, "You can't marry my son!"

This stuff was all new to me and I kept wondering why anyone cared.

**MARIE OSMOND BEGS GOD:** "HELP ME STAY A VIRGIN UNTIL MY WEDDING NIGHT"

**PHOTO SCREEN**

**PAUL MICHAEL GLA NAMED IN FARRAH DIVORCE SUIT!** Courtroom Testimon Shocks Lee!

**CHER AND "KISS" STAR SAY "I DO" IN SECRET CEREMONY!** Why She Left Her Honeymoon Bed In Tears!

From Beyond The Gra **ELVIS WARNS L "BEWARE TH NIGHT OF AUGUST** What He Fore On The Anni Of His Deat

# WHY ANYONE CARED

**Now It Can Be Told!**

**ELVIS SAVED JOHN TRAVOLTA'S LIFE!**
THE STRANGE LOVE CULT BOTH MEN HAD TO FIGHT!

NOV. • 75¢
Dell
U.K. 50p

## Modern Screen

MORE GOSSIP, PICTURES, FEATURES THAN EVER BEFORE!

**CHER** WARNED BY **KISS STAR'S** MOM: **"YOU CAN'T MARRY MY SON!"**

Cher Finds Out About His Secret Wife And Cries: **'NOW MY BABY WILL HAVE NO FATHER!'**

**FARRAH SNEAKS OFF TO FRANCE WITH NEW LOVE!**

**HER MOTHER & SISTER RUSH OVER TO SAVE HER FROM HEARTBREAK!** Why They Couldn't Keep The News From Lee!

**TWO ANGELS IN SURPRISE SOUTHERN WEDDING!**
• JACKIE & DENNIS SHARE VOWS IN CHURCH CEREMONY!
• KATE PROMISES NEW HUSBAND: 'OUR BABY COMES FIRST!'

---

**DONNY OSMOND: WE SINNED BEFORE OUR WEDDING NIGHT!**
He And His Bride Await First Baby!

OCT. • 75¢    IND 59553

PLUS TV

## movie MIRROR

**Cher Reveals: I'M GETTING MARRIED AGAIN!**

**CHASTITY THRILLED AS KISS STAR MOVES IN!** Nursery Prepared For New Baby!

**BURT & SLY STALLONE FIGHT OVER SALLY FIELD!**
How She Keeps Both Her Men Begging For More! **BURT TELLS SALLY: GIVE HIM UP OR WE'RE FINISHED!**

**SUZANNE SOMERS' SON RUSHED TO HOSPITAL!** Doctors Give Her Tragic News! SHE BEGS GOD TO KEEP HER CHILD ALIVE!

---

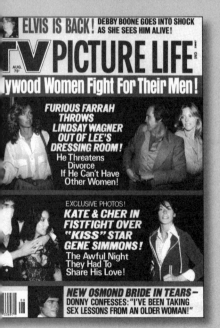

**ELVIS IS BACK!** DEBBY BOONE GOES INTO SHOCK AS SHE SEES HIM ALIVE!

AUG.
75¢

## TV PICTURE LIFE    IND

Hollywood Women Fight For Their Men!

**FURIOUS FARRAH THROWS LINDSAY WAGNER OUT OF LEE'S DRESSING ROOM!**
He Threatens Divorce If He Can't Have Other Women!

EXCLUSIVE PHOTOS!
**KATE & CHER IN FISTFIGHT OVER "KISS" STAR GENE SIMMONS!**
The Awful Night They Had To Share His Love!

**NEW OSMOND BRIDE IN TEARS—**
DONNY CONFESSES: "I'VE BEEN TAKING SEX LESSONS FROM AN OLDER WOMAN!"

---

**TRAVOLTA'S SECRET MARRIAGE DISCOVERED!**
WHY HE HIDES HIS BRIDE FROM THE WORLD!

OCT. 75¢

## TV & movie screen

**FARRAH WALKS IN ON LEE & NUDE BEAUTY!**
THE HEARTACHE THAT LEADS HER TO OTHER MEN! *DIVORCE PLANS CONFIRMED!*

**BURT LEAVES EXPECTANT SALLY IN DELIVERY ROOM!** *"I NEVER STOPPED LOVING DINAH!"* DINAH TELLS SALLY: "WE'LL GIVE YOUR CHILD A HOME!"

**CHER'S 'KISS' BOYFRIEND ADMITS: "I'VE SLEPT WITH 1,000 GIRLS!"** WHAT CHER DOES FOR HIM THAT OTHER WOMEN WON'T!

was once the Heart Fund building on 64th and Fifth in New York City, right across the street from the Children's Zoo. The building was only five stories high. On top of the fifth floor was nothing, only air. In New York City because land is limited, you can actually buy air rights. So I bought thirty-five feet of air rights and built a penthouse on 64th Street facing Fifth Avenue. I didn't have to dig into the ground, and the electricity and water were already hooked up, sparing me a great deal of expense. The actual cost of putting the penthouse up could have run into the millions, but it wound up costing about $500,000.

> # The consequences of not making sure you've taken care of this "business of marriage" before will soon be the painful realization that divorce will make short business out of you after!

The relationship between Cher and me eventually changed from romance to friendship. I then started a relationship with Diana Ross. I maintained my penthouse but would often spend days and weekends with Diana and her three wonderful children. We also agreed that what was hers was hers and what was mine was mine. I care for and respect Cher. I care for and respect Diana. But the cornerstone of caring and respect is honesty and full disclosure!

Life and the financial decisions you make for yourself do not stop at the doorway of marriage and relationships. The consequences of not making sure you've taken care of this "business of marriage" before will soon be the painful realization that divorce will make short business out of you after!

They don't teach you this, but love can be the most expensive part of your life. It might help you if you found out just how expensive "expensive" can be...*before* the relationship.

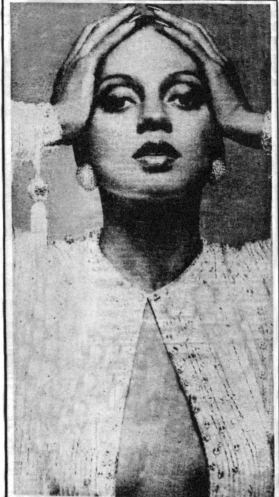

# Diana Ross has fallen for Cher's old beau Gene

*Kiss star Gene Simmons (above) with former lover Cher (below).*

By MARC KALECH

DIANA ROSS has a new boy friend — outrageous Kiss rock star Gene Simmons, Cher's lover until last year.

The beautiful pop singer revealed today that she's in love with Simmons — who never appears in public without his grotesque stage makeup.

"Gene's gorgeous . . . and very different off stage," Diana said in London.

"Under the paint, he is tall, dark and handsome. He's intelligent and an ex-teacher. He is so gentle, not a bit like the monster he looks like on stage."

According to the 36-year-old former lead singer for the Supremes, there was no competition for Simmons between her and Cher.

As a matter of fact, she said, she was introduced to Simmons by Cher at a surprise birthday party for the Kiss singer.

Diana, who is touring with Simmons on Kiss' current European tour, said she has no plans to make the singer her second husband.

Her first marriage ended in divorce four years ago.

"We have been together for three months but there is no talk of marriage yet," she said.

"We have a wonderful relationship. But we are completely different in every way."

# Again...

- Are you about to buy a new car?
  DON'T! (Do it later!)

- Are you about to buy a new house?
  DON'T! (Do it later!)

- Do you want to vacation and enjoy life
  now, or do you want to amass your
  fortune now and vacation later?

- Keep good records and keep your receipts.
  Give all of them to your accountant and
  tell him what they're for.

- If you're building an addition on your house
  you (hopefully) own or you're using a room
  as an office to conduct your business, you
  can deduct the cost or rent of that section.

- In simple terms, try not to buy anything...
  especially what you don't need.
  But if you buy, figure out a way to
  deduct the cost from your taxes.
  Get professional advice (not from me).

- Don't hang out with druggies...you will
  lose everything, but mostly money.

- Don't hang out with drinkers...same thing.

- Do get straight, if you're not.
  (Obvious, but worth saying.)

- Drinking and drugs will prevent you
  from making money. That's a promise.
  Something's gotta go. If you're like me
  and love money, get rid of all the monkeys
  on your back. *NOW!!*

# CHAPTER FIVE

# Changes

I've never been drunk in my life. I have never been high, except in a dentist's chair. I've never taken more than a sip or two of beer; I hate the taste and smell of it. I have never smoked, except for one or two puffs from a hidden pack of my mother's cigarettes when I was twelve years old. After that I never put another cigarette in my mouth again. I have never touched drugs. I've been a "good boy." I've worked hard. And *no one* is allowed the fruits of my labor without my permission.

I'm not saying this for effect, but as a for-your-information only. Now if you take a look at this very small idea, it's a personal choice I made, although convention and society actually espouse the notion of drinking. James Bond has his martinis, and Joe Middle America watches a Sunday football game and drinks brews as he yells, "Go Bears!" I just don't like the smell of alcohol or the taste of it—there's nothing about it that's appealing in the least.

> **I've never been drunk in my life. I have never been high, except in a dentist's chair.**

It also costs money, a lot of it. Drinking is not a solitary activity, unless you're a blatant drunk and have very bad self-esteem problems. Drinking is a social phenomenon. You like to drink beer or booze, and lots of it, because this is America and you like to do

> I haven't sat down and done the arithmetic, but I would imagine I've saved a small fortune simply by not drinking. Not to mention less aspirin tabs for headaches, no time lost from work due to hangovers... you do the math.

it with your buddies. And often you'll spring for the tab, because you're such a "man." That means that you'll be out a lot of cash, and you won't even have gotten a lap dance.

I haven't sat down and done the arithmetic, but I would imagine I've saved a small fortune simply by not drinking. Not to mention less aspirin tabs for headaches, no time lost from work due to hangovers...you do the math. I've also never been high in my life in any way, shape or form. I've never held a marijuana cigarette in my hand and have never stuck anything that looks remotely like Sweet 'n' Low up my nose. It's simply a personal choice. This doesn't make me very popular (in that way) at parties, because parties are based on the notion that people need to get blitzed in order to be effective at attracting the opposite sex.

> Sex, drugs and rock'n'roll. My favorite word, "sex," is right at the beginning.

I have worked for more than thirty years in an industry that actually espouses the lifestyle in a phrase we've all come to know and love dearly: Sex, drugs and rock'n'roll. My favorite word, "sex," is right at the beginning. There's that dreaded, self destructive word "drugs" right in the middle, and the rock 'n'roll part nobody can quite figure out. It seems harmless enough.

I'm here to tell you that a loser came up with that middle word, but clearly the industry is filled with mongoloids with guitars hanging around their necks. Because when this idiot was just a poor kid, before he got famous, he didn't have access to many drugs and may not have been a drug addict at all. He aspired to greatness and riches and as many women as he could get. And, of course, as soon as he got it, what did he do? He became a drug addict. His descent was hastened into a hell, behind a turnstile someplace, where he's doomed to ask—you guessed it—"Want fries with that?"

On tour with KISS, I would walk into a room. It would be filled with groupies. They would either be 1) drinking or 2) doing drugs. While everybody in that room was blitzed, I would simply walk in like the fox in the henhouse and take out all the chicks I liked. When the girls were with me—one, two or more—smoking was not allowed, drinking was not allowed and getting high was not allowed. For one thing, there are financial repercussions if someone is in your room and overdoses. Also, if she is drunk and/or high she might do something that will bring the law coming. At the end of the day, I never wanted to be around anyone who drank or got high. I was always, you might be surprised to know,

> **I chose a certain lifestyle: hard work, no drugs or booze and no marriage. It has served me well.**

much more interested in being around managers and record company people and, to be perfectly blunt, bankers. And if not entirely, then at least their sisters and girlfriends...

I chose a certain lifestyle: hard work, no drugs or booze and no marriage. It has served me well. You are free to choose your lifestyle! May it serve you as well as mine has served me!

# AVCO GIVES AUSTRALIA A GREAT BIG KISS!

# $152,204

### FIRST WEEK / 10 THEATRES IN SYDNEY, MELBOURNE, ADELAIDE AND BRISBANE

© Aucoin 1979 by agreement with KISS

**AND** KISS is a near capacity hit in 6 cities in Germany and in its initial opening in Holland!

You can't miss with KISS - the movie that has the whole world jumping!

## KISS in ATTACK OF THE PHANTOMS

A HANNA-BARBERA PRODUCTION in association with KISS-AUCOIN PRODUCTIONS
Starring PETER CRISS, ACE FREHLEY, GENE SIMMONS, PAUL STANLEY
Co-starring ANTHONY ZERBE, DEBORAH RYAN, CARMINE CARIDI Written by JAN-MICHAEL SHERMAN and DON BUDAY
Produced by TERRY MORSE, JR. Directed by GORDON HESSLER Executive Producer JOE BARBERA Executive Producer for KISS WILLIAM M. AUCOIN

### An International Release Through
**AVCO** EMBASSY PICTURES

When we made our movie of the week KISS Meets the Phantom of the Park (one of its titles), we knew next to nothing about the process. All we knew was that we would be in a KISS movie. It originally aired on Halloween on NBC-TV and actually did very well in viewership. It was a co-production between KISS and Hanna-Barbera, who were known primarily as cartoon makers (Flintstones, Scooby-Doo, etc.).

The movie was eventually sold to AVCO Embassy, a feature film company that then sold the film around the world theatrically. I remember during our 1979 tour of Canada, on one of our off days, I went to see the movie in a packed movie theater. And when we played Australia in 1980 I went to see the movie playing at a drive-in theater outdoors.

The film performed well, and AVCO took out a full-page ad in the international edition of Variety, the movie industry's trade publication. The film has since been waiting for someone to release it (legally) as a DVD. The rights issues haven't been all cleared through the years and may be lost in some back office somewhere. But not a day goes by when someone doesn't ask me when the DVD is coming.

\*     \*     \*

By 1980 the plan was to bring on our business manager, Howard Marks, to help us reduce our cost of doing business and maximize our bottom line, our profit. For a couple of years we watched our money grow, but not to the extent we were satisfied with.

Some real differences had started to surface between Bill Aucoin and the band. Aucoin always struck me as a man of vision. He could see the big picture. He was a showman in the grand tradition. He saw something in KISS that perhaps we didn't see in ourselves. He saw that we could go beyond just being a rock band and become superheroes if we chose to.

With all the wonderful creative ideas Bill Aucoin had, I have to say that financially he might not have been his own best advisor, or the band's. He lived way beyond his means. He had earned many millions of dollars from KISS and decided to open multiple offices on both coasts, New York and Los Angeles. His staff grew to two floors in New York on Madison Avenue and two floors in LA on Wilshire Boulevard. Additionally, he decided that his rented apartment on Fifth Avenue should have marble. After the lease was up, he couldn't take it with him. Hundreds of thousands of dollars of marble work remained in the apartment after he left.

One can live beyond one's means, or one can live right at the level of one's means. The problem with living beyond one's means is simply that there's no room for any flexibility. If the house of cards loses one card, the whole house comes tumbling down. Bill Aucoin had some brilliant ideas and was a man whose

> The **problem** with living beyond one's means is simply that there's no room for any flexibility. If the house of cards loses one card, the whole house comes **tumbling down.**

## What can I say about my partner?

He is the brother I never had. He's been the front man of the band since its inception.

When we first played the Daisy in Long Island in 1973, we hadn't yet figured out who was going to talk onstage. Peter tried it. Ace tried it. But Paul took to it immediately. And when we heard him, we knew he should be the voice of the band.

When I first met Paul, he didn't much like me. He thought I was full of myself—judgmental, perhaps even harsh. He's probably right. He's always been straight up with me. He's told me when I was full of it and has told me when I came up with the goods.

At first sight Paul and I seem alike in many ways. We both share a blue-collar work ethic. We are both driven people. But we are nonetheless as dif-

# PAUL STANLEY

ferent as night and day. I often use the following to illustrate my point: We both love chocolate cake. But Paul likes the frosting, whereas I like the devil's food cake (naturally).

Over the years he has stood up and drawn his own lines in the sand, and in retrospect, they have often turned out to be the right lines. By 1982 KISS had lost Peter and Ace. We released Creatures of the Night with two new members. The record and the ensuing tour didn't do well. We had played to stadiums in South America, and upon our return to America to record our follow-up album, Lick It Up, Paul tried to convince me to go at it without make-up. I thought he was wrong. He insisted. I gave in.

He was right.

He was so right that even without make-up and even with new members, KISS went on to sold-out tours and platinum albums. We were in hog heaven. At least I thought so. Paul wasn't so sure. He kept insisting that the business people who worked for us might not be doing what they were hired to do. He told me he was leaving the business managers, whether I came with him or not. He had drawn a line in the sand again. He brought in his own people who, after due diligence, offered some troublesome information: We owed the government millions of dollars in taxes and the band's pension was in deep trouble—in fact, it didn't exist.

He was right.

Because of his insistence, we were able to change a potentially damaging financial situation. We went on to a financial windfall with the new people involved in our affairs.

By the mid-90s, we had braved numerous personnel changes in the band. We had survived the stigma of KISS without make-up. We had survived and actually thrived without Ace and Peter. We weren't the number one band, but we were certainly doing well.

Paul thought it was time for KISS to do a Reunion Tour. Just like that.

He kept calling me and insisting we should talk to Ace and Peter. He thought they would do it. Because of the torture they had put us through, I thought it would never work. I was wrong.

He was right.

He's been right many times. He tends not to talk about it as much as I do. I tend to shoot my mouth off. He tends to go about things more quietly. I will boast of my sexual conquests; Paul will not. It's no secret the girls love Paul.

Over the years I'd have to say he has not gotten his due. Not from the fans. Not from the media. Most importantly, not from me.

We are two pieces of the same puzzle.

He completes me. I'd like to think I complete him.

Here's to my partner of thirty years... and counting—Paul Stanley.

By l982 we had released Creatures of the Night *using different guitar players. Ace was on his way out of the band. We toured with a new guitar player and did fairly poor business. Our support band was Wendy O. Williams and The Plasmatics. I was never fond of their songs but found myself fascinated by this girl who had a "take no prisoners" attitude in her stage shows. She would come out with a chain saw and go full steam at a television set. She didn't think twice of diving into the audience. She wore next to nothing, if she wore anything at all. She seemed completely comfortable in her own skin, and I started to wonder what it would be like to write some songs for her.*

*I had a few meetings with her manager, and we soon decided to make a record together. I agreed to produce under the following conditions: 1) She would let me pick who played on the record. I didn't think much of the musicianship in her band. This caused a little trouble for her, but my job was to make a better record than she had ever made, and if I was to do that, I needed better players. 2) I wanted the album to be called Wendy O. Williams, not The Plasmatics. The album would be called* Wow. *3) I would get to pick all the material. The songwriting within the band was limited. I wrote a few songs for them, found another and the band-written material was rearranged and reworked to suit the "new sound."*

*I then found different players to record the album. Even though Ace had left the band by this time, I called and asked him to come down and play a solo. He did. I asked Paul to come down and play. He did, I asked Eric Carr to come down. He did.*

*The album was released on a label that was going out of business, unfortunately. But the experience was terrific, and Wendy got the record she wanted.*

*The workload was enormous, but the pride in the work done was more than satisfying.*

vision helped take KISS to levels we might not have reached alone. After KISS and Bill Aucoin split up in 1982 he had a couple successes with other artists, and then reportedly lost all his money.

There were also deep divisions within the band by that time. Ace and Peter had been involved in something like ten separate car accidents. In more than one case the accidents resulted in extended hospital stays to treat life-threatening injuries. Cars caught fire, skidded more than 400 feet, swiped off other car doors; there were races in DeLoreans at over 100 miles an hour, arrests for illegal drug prescriptions, gun-carrying on airlines...there were endless variations on these themes, all of which in one way or the other eventually led to Peter and Ace being out of the band.

Peter left first in 1980, then Ace departed in 1982. Both went on to pursue solo careers; both failed and had to declare bankruptcy. Eventually, by 1993, Ace and Peter were co-headlining a club tour called "Bad Boys of Rock." Neither one on their own could fill a club.

KISS continued without them. We had a new album to record called *Creatures of the Night*. For a second, I thought Edward Van Halen should be our new guitarist when he and I met for lunch and he suggested it. It was not to be.

KISS was now Paul, Eric Carr, Vinnie Vincent and Gene Simmons. We toured with the new lineup and did relatively poor business. Our opening act was Wendy O. Williams. She and I agreed to do a record together that I would write and produce. The record failed, but this time I got paid.

I was invited to film an ABC-TV pilot for my own TV series called *Grotus*, featuring a jet-setting, skirt chasing guy...the creators were Marcy Carsey and her company Carsey-Werner, who would go on to do *Roseanne* and *The Cosby Show*. I passed the audition, met the ABC brass and was offered the show. Their first offer was $60,000 an episode. I was elated.

I was told they would need me fulltime for ten months a year. That meant no touring and no records. It would actually cost me money to do the series. I would be paying for the privilege of starring on a television show, because I'd have to take a sabbatical from KISS, which would cost me millions.

I wanted to expand my areas of interest, but only if it made me money. I like fame as much as the next guy, but you can't pay your rent with it. Remember, it's "rich and famous," not "famous and rich."

This is not to discount the importance of celebrity in our culture. If your aspirations are to become Shaq or Tiger Woods, your chances are slim. If you spent your entire life training since the time you were a child to become a super-athlete, and if you actually scale the heights and become Tiger Woods, you may be shocked to find out no matter how lucrative (in the millions of dollars) your payday may be, you can earn multiple times the gross number of dollars you're paid in intangibles like TV advertisements and product endorsements. In fact, what you're being paid for is *being famous.* Not for the actual work you do. Fame in and of itself is something to aspire to! The reward and consequence of fame is often money—sometimes truckloads!

> **Fame** in and of itself is something to aspire to! The reward and consequence of fame is often **money**— sometimes truckloads!

America doesn't have royalty; since we don't have kings and queens, we don't actually heap billions of dollars on them for doing nothing, American royalty is celebrity-hood itself. We have stars on the Hollywood Walk of Fame (KISS has one), not just in the heavens above us. We not only lavish praise and money, but give lots of free stuff to people just because they're famous.

When I was no one, I never got a free meal or a free bus ride—and make no mistake about it, I would have appreciated one. When I didn't have money, I would have loved to get a free meal. But as soon as I became famous, on whatever level I achieved fame, everyone—restaurants, clothing-makers, guitar manufacturers—wanted to give me free stuff, and lots of it. Just because I was famous.

It's come to the point now where people just want me to show up and speak! They're called "lectures," but what it really comes down to is that I show up someplace, somebody gives me sackfuls of cash and I start talking. It's very stream-of-consciousness. I usually open with "I was very young when I was born." I don't have a clue where the next sentence is coming from or where I will end up, but at the end of the day what it's really about is they're waiting for me to stop talking. They want me to jump into the audience and take questions, and then pose for photos. They want to be with me just because of celebrity-hood.

> When I was no one, I never got a free meal or a free bus ride—and make no mistake about it, I would have appreciated one. When I didn't have money, I would have loved to get a free meal.

I never take any of this seriously. I'm as amazed by the power of celebrity as you are. It's important to be aware of its power.

In 1985, we went out on tour. We always toured. Our opening band this time was Black 'N Blue. We struck up a friendship and started talking about recording a record together. Eventually I wound up producing two albums for the Geffen Records band. The process of being in a studio with another band opened my eyes to the different sides of the music business. You could get paid by another band for producing them. You could write for another band and get paid royalties for your songwriting and publishing. And then there were the intangibles—you dealt with record company executives on a different level.

I had grown close to lead singer Jamie St. James and guitarist-songwriter Tommy Thayer. They were hard workers, and I always respected that. Thayer in particular struck me as someone who could go further than the band he was in. I wasn't sure yet what that meant, but over the years my sense of the possibilities within certain people have usually turned out to be right.

Thayer kept in touch with me, even as his band was about to break up. We started writing songs together—some of which wound up on KISS records. Again, his professionalism shined. He would make an appointment and show up on time. This was an anomaly, as far as most musicians went. He didn't hang out. He didn't drink. He didn't smoke. He wanted to make it, but didn't know what that meant. Neither did I. But I had the sense he could. It would take a few more years for me to put all the pieces of the Tommy Thayer puzzle together. But, eventually it would become clear.

Even though I had scaled the heights with KISS, I often wondered if this rat only knew its way through one maze. Or, was I any good at other areas as well.

By this time, I had amassed a decent amount of money. I was debt-free. I always was. I owned my own land. And even though KISS toured and recorded more often than other bands, free time on my hands was not something I enjoyed. I had never taken a real vacation. I never wanted one. I simply enjoyed working too much.

Peter Criss had been out of the band, by this point, for over five years. The guys in Black 'N Blue wanted to invite him to sing on one of the songs. I called him and he was glad to come down. The recording session went well. Peter's career had stalled years earlier. He didn't have a record contract. He couldn't tour because there wasn't a demand for him. I hoped this recording session would pick up his spirits.

As it turned out, I wouldn't see again Peter for another ten years —1995, the Reunion Tour.

# Record Producer

I tried producing other bands. Virgin was a Bill Aucoin-managed band. It failed. I discovered another band and had them signed to Casablanca. They were called Group With No Name (their name choice) and featured Katey Sagal, who would later become famous on *Married With Children*. It failed. I produced a group called Smashed Gladys. They eventually signed with Elektra Records. It failed.

I had tried producing and writing songs for other bands. I had tried television. I was about to try movies.

# Movie Producer

Nothing comes to you! You have to go to it! I wanted to act, noticed a casting company called Fenton and Feinberg and called them. Mike Fenton must have been surprised to hear me introduce myself and offer: "I want to be in movies."

## Nothing comes to you! You have to go to it!

We met, he introduced me to writer-director Michael Crichton and in short order I was cast as the bad guy Luther in Tri-Star Films' *Runaway*. A few hundred thousand dollars later, I was looking forward to more film work.

In 1984, we started working on a new album called Asylum. For a few years I had been doing research into the movie industry. I had delusions of grandeur. I thought I could act. Maybe I can and maybe I can't, but I was going to give it a try. I have to admit my interest in movies ran so deep that I was reading The Hollywood Reporter and Daily Variety (the movie industry trade publications), even while we were in the studio recording various albums or out on tour. Everyone around me was mystified as to why I was doing this. But I was headstrong and determined.

Before the recording got underway, I picked up the phone, called information, found the number of Fenton and Feinberg, a casting agency in Hollywood, and phoned them out of the blue. I had noticed their name in numerous movie end credits. I spoke with Mike Fenton. I said I was Gene Simmons and that I wanted to be in movies. Not the best introduction, I'll grant you, but Mike was kind enough to invite me down to their offices that afternoon.

I sat in with Mike and his partner and, within a few minutes, he made a phone call which brought me face to face with Michael Crichton, who was about to write and direct a motion picture called Runaway, a title I never liked. He introduced me to his producer Mike Rachmil, and after a few moments of pleasantries, Crichton asked me to stare into his eyes for thirty seconds without making faces or grimacing. I didn't know why, but after I came up for air, he told me I had the part if I wanted it.

The part was Luther, an evil scientist. They were going to shoot in Vancouver, Canada in the summer, and I had to commit. I did. This would interfere with our New York recording sessions, however. I told the band

**RUNAWAY**          A Tri-Star Picture

*about it and the response was not good. I had the opportunity, and I wasn't going to let it go.*

*Paul, despite his displeasure, took control of the studio recording process, even though we had yet another new guitarist in the band. We weren't sure he would be permanent; he had yet to have his baptism by fire on tour with us. We didn't know if he could cut it. He had some problems in the studio, mostly in slowing the speed of his guitar playing down so that it didn't sound like an angry bee. He also didn't have the ability to play the same passage more than once. Either way, I left New York after I had done all my lead vocals. Paul was left to flesh out the rest of the album—put on the backgrounds, the guitar solos, oversee the mixing, etc.*

*I cut my hair, flew up to Canada and gave it my best. Movies were like nothing I had ever been in contact with. The rock-and-roll pace was fast. Movies crawled. You would be on a set for twelve to sixteen hours, but most of the time was spent waiting for them to call you, so you could read your lines and be on camera for a few minutes.*

*Cast members included Tom Selleck, who starred; Cynthia Rhodes and Kirstie Alley, who played my girlfriend and whom I reluctantly stabbed through the base of her skull with a knife (in the movie—not in real life).*

*The movie was released by Tristar Pictures and we went out on tour.*

*Although I was paid six figures to be in the movie, I didn't quit my day job. I always had the philosophy, and still do, that having my cake was OK, but being able to eat it as well was preferable.*

I met two comic book writers, Jeph Loeb and Matt Weissman, at the Beverly Hills Hotel and we came up with an idea for a movie about an Israeli Mossad (CIA-type) agent whose little girl is kidnapped. I took the finished script to *Runaway's* producer as a starring vehicle for me. I was told it wasn't good—that it was just a lot of shooting. I let go of the script. But when I wanted to take another shot at it, it was too late. It was being made starring Arnold Schwarzenegger, using my title: *Commando*. Lesson learned. Again! Trust your gut. Not someone else's. Ask for other people's opinions, but follow your heart.

I found another script and got a free option for six months. I tried to set it up at the studios. They said it couldn't be made. The following year I went to see it in a movie theater. It was called *Jacob's Ladder*, directed by Adrian Lyne.

I tried to produce *The Deed*, a book by Gerold Frank. I was able to attach director Bruce Beresford (*Driving Miss Daisy*). I sold it to Warner Bros. Pictures. It has yet to be made.

The same goes for *The Neal Bogart Story* (Paramount)... *Sex Drugs and Rock 'n' Roll* (Touchstone)...*Jon Sable* (Intermedia/Pacifica)...*Tennessee Waltz* and *November Files* (Interlight) ...*Monster Truckin'* (7 Arts)...*Stupid Action Movie* (AMG)...*Real Monsters* (New Line)...*Groupies* (New Line)...

And on TV: *Gene Simmons Chillerama* (MTV)...*Hit Men* (VH1)...*Vox* (VH1)...*Smash* (VH1)...*My Dad the Rock Star* cartoon (Nelvana)...*Groupies* (movie of the week)...*Groupies* documentary (HBO)...*Rock and Roll All Nite* (CBS)...

Few, if any, will ever see the light of day. If it was easy, everyone would be doing it!

# Simmons Records

I had missed out on Van Halen and I desperately wanted my own label for new acts I discovered.

I got one. RCA President Bob Buziak and International President Heinz Henn gave me my own label—Simmons Records. RCA would pay me a six-figure overhead fee. They also paid for everything else— recording costs, artist advances, marketing and sales. I would participate on the profits of every record sold on my label.

I started using a logo I had trademarked six years earlier: the moneybag logo. I had started to put two slashes through the "S" in Simmons to resemble a dollar sign (which, if you haven't noticed by now, is very important to me and, I suspect, to you). I trademarked it. But it occurred to me that the universal sign for good fortune, the American dream, was the moneybag logo. I didn't believe I could ever own it. Surely someone had already trademarked it. They had not. I did!!!

I was even able to legally enforce it. A band by the name of Teenage Fan Club on Geffen Records used the moneybag on one of their album covers. I "cease and desisted" them (made them stop), they sent me a small check and the logo was forever mine.

> But it occurred to me that the universal sign for good fortune, the American dream, was the moneybag logo. I didn't believe I could ever own it. Surely someone had already trademarked it. They had not. I did!!!

In the late 70s, we all started to perfect our signatures. Initially someone would ask for my autograph and I wouldn't think twice about how to sign my name. I was too excited that someone wanted me to sign my name on a piece of paper to begin with to worry about what it looked like. I had taken such a great leap of faith in the first place by simply changing my name from Gene Klein to Gene Simmons that it never occurred to me that how my signature looked might be important.

I started signing my last name, Simmons, with two slashes through the "S." It make it look like a dollar sign. I liked it. I was never ashamed of wanting riches. It was the American Dream, after all. I wanted to be completely upfront about it. I noticed fans started signing their name with dollar signs through their names as well. If their last names started with a "C" then the "cent" sign would be the result.

It made me start thinking about the whole issue of who else can put slashes through their last names. So, management trademarked our signatures when we started to manufacture necklaces and the like featuring only our signatures. So, there it was. "Gene $immons" was a trademark.

I also wondered if anyone owned the "$" sign. I found out there were strict limitations on its use-ownership. But what would happen if I altered the design somewhat? The moneybag logo, for instance. Who owned it? I did a search, and found out no one owned it.

I trademarked the moneybag logo for paper goods, licensing and merchandising and other uses. All this meant that no one else (without my permission) could use the logo.

I eventually used the logo for: Simmons Records, my Punisher and Axe bass guitars, my Man of 1,000 Faces, Inc. company, GENE SIMMONS TONGUE magazine, my upcoming Gene Simmons clothing line and so on.

In the late 80s a Geffen group called Teenage Fan Club (which was quite good, actually) used my logo as the cover of their album. I sent a "cease and desist" letter and was elated to find that Geffen Records did not contest my ownership. They sent me a nice little check, and I had a paper trail bolstering my ownership of the logo.

It was the thrill of a lifetime to got this piece of paper from the United States Patent and Trademark Office. More paperwork was to follow, but eventually I got the trademark.

TRADEMARK

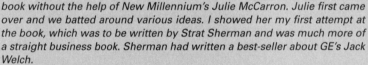

Here is the Simmons Records logo. I eventually used it on jackets and T-shirts and sold them in another state. Interstate commerce is one of the cornerstones of protecting one's trademark.

The book you're holding in your hand is published by Simmons Books/New Millennium Press, a joint venture. I met New Millennium head Michael Viner through producer Scott Steindorff. I liked what they published, and we immediately agreed to work together. He also brought up his "books on tape" division, and Simmons Audio was born.

A company is only as good as the people in the company. I couldn't have written this book without the help of New Millennium's Julie McCarron. Julie first came over and we batted around various ideas. I showed her my first attempt at the book, which was to be written by Strat Sherman and was much more of a straight business book. Sherman had written a best-seller about GE's Jack Welch.

When Julie and I first met, it was classic. She couldn't believe half the things that were coming out of my mouth (I'm sure half the time she thought they were coming out of my ass). And, the more shocked she was at what I was saying, the more convinced I became that what I had to do was to tell the truth (as I knew it)—with humor, but still stick to the truth. Because, hard as it was for Julie to swallow what I had to say, when pressed, she had to admit she didn't have a comeback. She would contend that while she respected my "outlandish" thoughts about the nature of men and women, she didn't think they reflected what most men thought.

They do.

Because of Julie, and because I enjoyed kidding around with her about how women generally live in a fantasy regarding the true nature of men (a woman might exclaim "You want me to put WHAT?? WHERE??" or "What are you doing back there????"), I found my "voice"—the tone the book should have.

Humorous. At least in intent. But hard-hitting in content and truthfulness.

Everything I wrote in here is true. For me, it's all true. I contend it's also true for most men. Privately, women might have to concede it's true. But, publicly they will not.

"Yes. I know men are that way. But not MY boyfriend."

Yes, he is.

I've already met with Viner about two other books we plan to publish. I'm having a ball on this new journey, and I thank you for giving me the opportunity.

# Billboard
NEWSPAPER

VOLUME 100   NO. 34   THE INTERNATIONAL NEWSWEEKLY OF MUSIC AND HOME ENTERTAINMENT   A

# Kiss' Gene Simmons Debuts Label
## Moneybag Logo Gets BMG Distribution

BY CHRIS MORRIS

LOS ANGELES "There's gold in them there hills, and I'm going to go dig it out," says Kiss bassist Gene Simmons, who has embarked on a new career as a record mogul with the creation of Simmons Records.

Simmons' label, distributed worldwide exclusively by BMG, will make its in-store bow in mid-September with the debut album by House Of Lords, a new hard rock quintet featuring former members of Camel/MCA act Giuffria. Andy Johns, who scored with his work with Cinderella, co-produced the album with band leader Greg Giuffria.

Other Simmons signings include Loz Netto, ex-guitarist for Sniff 'N' the Tears and a former Atlantic Records solo artist, who Simmons describes as an "English funkmeister"; Silent Rage, a Hawthorne, Calif.-based rock act with one album to its credit on Chameleon; and Jenny Muldaur, daughter of pop-folk singer Maria Muldaur.

So why has Simmons, already busy with multiple careers as a rock star, film actor, and artist manager (he handles Liza Minnelli and Karla DeVito), started his own label?

"It's real simple," he says. "Everybody's gone through this in their life—it's 'Gee, I wish I would have done that.' I'd rather try something and fail miserably than later on say I wish I would have tried it."

Simmons has unearthed some top talent in the past, but because of some less-than-farsighted advice he never managed to bring his discoveries to fruition at the major labels. For instance, Van Halen was originally signed exclusively to Simmons in the '70s; he produced the band's first demos.

"My then-manager, who has obviously since been fired, said that this group was too close to Black Oak Arkansas and they should go back to the hills where they came from," Simmons says. "I figured he must know something I don't, so I let them go."

Similarly, Simmons found Cinderella when the group submitted a demo tape to him.

"[I] took them into the regime at PolyGram at this time and said, 'This is going to be a big band,' and I was told they were not. I figured, well, they're in the record business, they know what I don't.

"Six months later the regime changed, and then Jon Bon Jovi went to see the band live and came back with reports about this stellar group, and then the new regime signed them."

Reflecting on these experiences, Simmons adds with a chuckle, "The idea for Simmons Records is very similar to [that of the Jewish Defense League]— Never again.' No more listening to people—it's trusting your gut and going for it."

Surprisingly, in view of Simmons' long career in heavy metal, he is not styling his label simply as a metal outlet.

"I like everything," he says. "I like radio, I like underground radio, I like college and alternative stuff ... There are no rules except what your ears dictate, period. As exemplified by the roster so far—I've got one pop act, one funk-urban act, and two rock acts, and both rock acts hopefully are different from one another."

The model for Simmons Records is a surprising one: "I'm not approaching it as Swan Song Records or Rolling Stones Records. This is patterned much more after Motown Records ... If I'm trying to copy [anything], it's Berry Gordy's vision, which is start with good songs and then you find the right artists to do it."

Still, Simmons Records' ultimate objective is probably defined by its corporate logo: "It's a money bag. You've seen guards take it into banks all the time. Mine's a silver money bag, for platinum."

In addition to his label venture, Simmons says he is still very much an active member of Kiss. In recent weeks, the band has been in New York cutting two new tracks, "Let's Put The X In Sex" and "Rock Hard," which the bassist says will be featured on a greatest-hits album, "Smashes, Thrashes, & Hits," to be released at the end of October.

On the concert front, Kiss was scheduled to play two special dates, Aug. 12-13, at Manhattan's Ritz club before heading to Europe for a series of Monsters Of Rock festival appearances. When the European trip ends, Simmons says the group will start work on a new studio project, the group's 23rd album.

*Assistance in preparing this story provided by Steve Gett in New York.*

---

By 1988, I wanted to branch out. I had been in KISS. We had reached the top. I found out that I would be allowed to act in movies. I was allowed to produce other rock bands. Because of that experience, I started getting the notion that perhaps I should have my own label. Reach for the stars, my mother would say. Those words ring true even today.

My first real thoughts about a label centered around a song I had written for my solo album Radioactive. "Radioactive" was a term commonly used in the industry to mean that a song was "active," or being played on the radio. I also liked the double entendre—the dangerous sound of it. I trademarked the name and started doodling designs. But I soon found pragmatism and my ego getting the better of me. Didn't I think "Simmons Records" sounded better than "Radioactive?"

I initially approached KISS' own label, Polygram. Although they were very nice to me, the result was a soft "no." I called a few other labels (if at first you don't succeed) and found a willing listener in RCA Records president Bob Buziak and VP Heinz Henn. Both supported the idea of a Simmons Records. I couldn't believe it.

We sat down and started to design the "voice" of the label. Would it be a "rock label" or would it be a general all-purpose label?

By that time I had started managing the musical career of Liza Minnelli. That happened as a result of our friendship. I wanted Liza to be my premier signing, but Buziak balked. I then took Liza over to CBS Records president Walter Yetnikoff who gave Liza a record deal on the spot. She would go on to record the most successful record of her career, featuring songs written and produced by the Pet Shop Boys.

I also started managing the daughter of Warner Bros. artist Maria Muldaur—Jenni Muldaur. I wanted to sign Jenni to my label. Buziak didn't buy it. So she wound up on Warner Bros. records. I also liked an English artist named Loz Netto, but Buziak didn't buy that one either.

I had run into Gregg Guiffria years earlier when he was in a band called Angel. The band was playing in a Washington, D.C. club in the mid-70s when we came down to see them. I was so impressed that during one of their breaks I got on the phone with our own Casablanca Records president Neal Bogart and raved about the band. He soon signed them. The band was always very thankful for that. So when I ran into Giuffria and he told me about his MCA records band Guiffria that was looking for another label, and after he played me a few of the songs, I told him I was interested. But only under the following terms: 1) There would have to be a name change. I could neither pronounce nor spell the name of the band. It sounded like a foreign exchange program from Italy. For pragmatic reasons, I didn't think it was commercial-sounding to American ears. 2) I would be able to pick the producers, the songs and even have something to say about their videos and stage shows. I had studied and admired Motown head Berry Gordy. He never let a single area of an artist get by him, unlike most record companies, who only concerned themselves with whether an artist had a hit single on the record. The name of the group would be changed to House of Lords (I had trademarked and owned the name earlier. I let the band use it without charging a royalty. But if the band broke up, the name would revert to me. I still own the name.) They were my premier release. They did reasonably well.

The second group came to me accidentally. One of the demos I heard was from a California group called Silent Rage. Although they didn't fare very well, they did wind up on a Black Sabbath tour. I was able to call the Sabbath management and ask for a favor.

The third group, Gypsy Rose, was given to me by Buziak. He wanted to sign them but thought they would have more credibility on Simmons Records than RCA records, which at that time didn't have rock acts. Ironic, since they were the home of Elvis Presley.

For practical reasons, and because I didn't want to waste any of the money I was given as "yearly overhead" (high six figures), I simply worked out of my guest house. I met all the bands there. I kept all the paperwork there. I also used no assistants. I made my own phone calls and went to my own meetings. Marketing, manufacturing and distribution would be done by RCA. I kept most of the money I made.

And, in case you're wondering, I didn't give up my day job. I was in KISS. I had Simmons Records. I managed Liza Minnelli. I acted in movies and produced other bands...time permitting, of course.

# Gene Simmons Takes a Spin as a Record Mogul

By PATRICK GOLDSTEIN

*Gene Simmons . . .*
*a mogul in Kiss make up?*

What worlds are left for Gene Simmons to conquer?

He's survived 22 Kiss albums (15 have gone platinum says Simmons, who keeps count), headlined concerts everywhere, embarked on an acting career (largely as a Hollywood heavy), romanced everyone from Cher and Diana Ross to Playmate Shannon Tweed and emerged as one of the elder statesmen of the heavy-metal underworld.

Now Simmons wants to be a record mogul. He's formed his own label, Simmons Records, and signed an exclusive distribution deal with RCA Records, which will market and distribute his artists here and overseas.

"I've discovered several big bands but never had anything to show for it because I've always listened to someone else, who *didn't* want to sign them," Simmons said.

Simmons has already signed one group, House of Lords, whose debut album is due out in September. But the voluble Kiss frontman—he's the kind of guy who *brags* that his band has never been favorably reviewed in Rolling Stone—insists that Simmons Records is more than just a vanity label.

"The label is very much patterned on the Berry Gordy-Clive Davis school of hands-on management," he explained. "I'm going to be involved in choosing the songs, production choices, arrangements—everything. If a group wanted to just make a record and hand it in, they probably shouldn't be at my label. But if there's any flak, I'll take that too. And I'll be accessible—you won't have to go through a bunch of secretaries to get to me."

As if to prove that he means business, Simmons has designed his own logo for the label—a pair of armored-car money bags, emblazoned with dollar signs. Tacky, you say?

"Make of it what you will," he retorted. "If you think it's decadent and corporate, that's fine. I'm going for the gold. Actually, make that the platinum!"

Simmons isn't kidding about taking control. House of Lords was originally known as Giuffria, but Simmons replaced the group's original lead singer—and changed its name. "I wanted something that sounded classy, and not too heavy-metal."

In the past, artist-run vanity labels—whether Elton John's Rocket Records or the Jefferson Airplane's Grunt Records—have been financial flops. But industry insiders praise Simmons' good business sense and shrewd talent-scout instincts. (And wide-ranging pop interests—he also manages Liza Minnelli, who has just signed to Elektra Records).

"Gene has great instincts about what kind of bands teen-agers like to hear," said Geffen A&R exec John Kalodner. "The big question is—how much time can he put into this, considering that he's also in a very successful rock band? Being a record exec is a 24-hour-a-day job. But he has good ears—he'll be just as good at finding new groups as any A&R guy that's at CBS Records these days."

Simmons isn't shy about recounting his discoveries. He says he signed a management deal with Van Halen after finding them playing in a local dive. "I paid for their demo record, flew them to New York—I even bought David Lee Roth his first pair of leather pants," he said. "But my manager told me they'd never make it, that Roth looked too much like Jim Dandy. So I let 'em go."

He says he also first brought Cinderella to PolyGram Records, but "no one running the company then" wanted to sign them. "That's the idea behind this new label," he said. "No more listening to anyone else."

Simmons said he originally offered to affiliate his label with PolyGram (where Kiss is signed), but the company balked at certain contractual stipulations, particularly Simmons' insistence that each new band would be guaranteed videos to promote their albums.

So now he's at RCA, which will release at least three other Simmons groups over the next eight months. "We're gonna do all kinds of music—I'm not interested in just signing some group called the Kill Brigade," he said. "And we're going to be very budget conscious. No limos, no million-dollar recording sessions. I've been there before, so I know all the angles. Don't count on anyone fooling me."

□

*Silent Rage*

# Manager

My friendship with Liza Minnelli resulted in a management contract for her recording career. I offered Liza as my first artist on
Simmons Records. It was rejected. So I took her to Walter
Yetnikoff at CBS who put her on Epic Records. Her Pet Shop Boys-
written-and-produced album was a gold record overseas and did
moderately well in America.

I also had Jenni Muldauer, who eventually went to Warner
Records; Loz Netto, Dead or Alive and others. All rejected. But
Greg Guiffria's new band, House of Lords, whose name I dubbed
and owned, worked. They recorded two records for me. I also
released Silent Rage and Gypsy Rose on Simmons Records.

I produced a Japanese band, Ezo, for Geffen Records, as well as two
albums for Black 'N Blue (Geffen) and two albums for Keel (A&M).

Most of the ventures I undertake fail. So will yours. So what!
Get used to being immune to the word "NO" and the concept of
failure. "If at first you don't succeed, try, try again." Good words to
live by. For me. For you.

\*　　\*　　\*

As I looked toward California in 1984, I decided to sell my New York place. I sold it for almost *six times* what I'd bought it for only two years earlier. The laws of real estate at that time said that whatever earned income (capital gains) you had from a house, you could hold onto for two years tax-free. At that point you either had to buy another house for the exact amount of the selling price within two years, or get a tax bill for the differential. As it happened, within a year or two of selling I was able to turn the profits from the sale of my penthouse and almost double that money on Wall Street.

I met Shannon Tweed, a former *Playboy* Playmate of the Year. She certainly had beauty and brains, but there was something more: I liked being with her. Once I sold my place in New York I came west and moved into Shannon's apartment in LA. She was sharing it with her sister and a male roommate. Her total rent was probably $800 a month. I was by no means living at the top end of my financial means. Eventually I decided that I wanted to buy a house on two acres in Beverly Hills. I built a guesthouse on the property that served, for all intents and purposes, as the KISS West Coast office and headquarters for Simmons Records.

It looked like the relationship with Shannon was going to be a "go." We were approaching our second year together. I told Shannon, "I want to be clear. I said this to you when we first started the relationship and I'll say it again now. I never want to get married. If we're going to live together, I want a cohabitation agreement. Not a pre-nup. I don't want anyone besides you and I, Shannon Tweed and Gene Simmons (with the help of individual counsel) to decide what the nature of our relationship is."

And to her credit she agreed. She got her own lawyer and I got my own lawyer and we both wrote down our wish list. I wrote that I cared deeply for her and wanted to live with her, but never wanted to have joint credit card and bank accounts. I wasn't looking for

Jon Sable *is a comic book by Mike Grell. In 1986 I was offered the lead role for a TV movie of the week pilot by director Gary Sherman. Sherman had directed me in New World's* Wanted: Dead or Alive.

*Sable, as the legend goes, was born and raised in the wilds of Africa. His father was a game warden. Sable grows up in the jungle and eventually his family is killed. He comes to America and becomes a "big game hunter in the concrete jungle." A hero for hire.*

*I flew to Chicago and landed during one of the worst winter storms to film the pilot. My costar was Rene Russo, who had just switched from modeling to acting. She would go on to act opposite Mel Gibson, Pierce Brosnan and others.*

*Within a week of filming I found out they intended to turn* Jon Sable *into a weekly adventure TV series. I had assumed it was going to be a few TV movies of the week. I wanted to stay in the band and, in my "off time," I also wanted to act. The reality was becoming clearer—it looked as if it just wouldn't work into my schedule.*

*I also wasn't very good in the part.*

*They paid me off and I left the project. They hired another actor and* Sable *saw the light of day on ABC for six episodes.*

*In 1999 I was at Golden Apple (a comic book store) and went looking for* Jon Sable *comics. I couldn't find them. But someone suggested I contact another store and, once I got my hands on the comic books, I decided to try to get the rights. I did. I convinced creator Mike Grell and his lawyer that if I couldn't get the project set up as a motion picture within a short time, they could have the rights back.*

*I pitched* Sable *to Pacifica (Intermedia), who were eventually to release the Harrison Ford* K-19: The Widowmaker *film, and they bought it. We thought Steven De Souza (of* Die Hard *and* Predator *fame) could write the script. They didn't want to pay De Souza inflated writer's fees, so I offered my services to negotiate. Steven and I talked straight, and in a short time all parties agreed. We talked about Pierce Brosnan as Sable. The script had three rewrites and eventually went into "turnaround"—it was never made and the rights reverted back.*

*But one day* Sable *will see the light of day.*

a partner, and I didn't want to be her partner. Whatever bank accounts Shannon had, I didn't want to know about! I didn't want to know how much she had or where she kept her money. It was none of my business. She earned that money. Likewise, she would have nothing to say about my finances.

I was completely honest from the first day we got together. I told Shannon, "I will never get married. I will never marry any woman. I want to be free to decide whatever I want to do with my life, and likewise, I will never tell you where to go or what to do. There are no preconditions for us living together except for one: If we break up, you take what was yours, and I will likewise take what was mine. This relationship is not about money. It is about companionship. If we ever do have children, they will be my responsibility."

We're approaching twenty years together: We both signed the contracts. My biggest wish was for complete honesty and full disclosure. I strongly urge everybody to sign such papers *before* entering any kind of romantic relationship. This means you!

It's possible that at any point one person or the other in a relationship will change. It's not even necessarily that one is a villain and the other is a saint. The problem with all relationships is the financial cost when you "change." You can walk out on your friends when you change; you can even walk out on your parents! But you can't walk out on somebody you lived with—not without paying them more money than the one who gave you life itself, your mother. It's the law of the land...unless you have a binding agreement that supersedes and nullifies it! Like I do!

> You can walk out on your friends when you change; you can even walk out on your parents! But you can't walk out on somebody you lived with— not without paying them more money than the one who gave you life itself, your mother.

# Again...

- Nothing will come to you! You have to go after it! Remember, if it was easy, everybody would be doing it.

- Do you want marriage...or not?
  Do you want freedom...or not?

- Are your romantic relationships based on honesty and full disclosure?

# CHAPTER SIX

# Women are From Mars... Men Have Penis

've often joked privately that marriage is an institution. You have to be committed to it. If that doesn't sound like a nuthouse, I don't know what does.

Or try this one on for size: What do women do with their assholes? They send them to work.

A man mutters a few words in church and finds himself married. He mutters a few words in his sleep and finds himself divorced.

Before marriage, a man yearns for the woman. After marriage the "Y" becomes silent.

Women are from Mars...men have penis. That's about as close as we get to each other.

The road to riches for men and women are two completely different paths that never touch. What's good for the goose is not necessarily good for the gander, and vice versa. Women want life partners. I don't know about you, but I'm not looking for a partner—a financial partner, that is. I already have one. It's called the United States government (whether I want it to be or not). I have to pay tax dollars; I refuse to tithe to churches. I don't want to pay for the privilege of praying to God, and I don't want to pay for the privilege of companionship. But my hand is not out looking for money from anyone else, either! I'm sure there are some women who agree with me. The majority do not.

My life, by example, I hope, is duly diligent. I'm told it's not a very romantic notion, but I'm here to tell you that marriage isn't necessarily the most financially beneficial institution for a man. Romance is financially beneficial for a woman, however. Romance and love are "blinding" AND "binding." There's a reason people say "Love is blind." It doesn't deal with consequences, it says dive into the deep end of the pool. Because women have nothing to lose (financially speaking) and everything to gain. At least that's the law of our land. I'm not making a value judgment. You decide for yourself.

> # Romance and love are "blinding" AND "binding." There's a reason people say "Love is blind."

# The Myth of Love

Let's examine "love" for a little longer. We're taught that love is everything. It's not. That is a myth, it is a patent lie. Say you're a Third World woman in the Kalahari desert somewhere in Africa, and your child is starving to death, God forbid. You're holding your child in your arms as he is dying. You say to your child, "I love you." I don't know how to dispel anybody's notions about the power of even motherly love, but it means nothing at that moment. The very first and foremost thing you need—above civilization and laws and religion and God—is food and air. The basics. Air is free. Food is not. You need money. More is better than less. After money, you may want love. But love is not necessary for survival and is certainly far from "the most powerful force in the world," despite what we're taught.

What we're taught in America about love in song lyrics is completely untrue. "How can I live without you?" "Love is everything." It's not! Love is, in fact, often abused and used as a weapon of sorts.

The last thing I want is to be loved by someone who doesn't love themselves! I want to be around somebody who's richer than I am. I want to be around somebody who's smarter than I am. I don't want to be around somebody who's dumber than I am or loves themselves less than I do. Anyone who loves themselves less than I love myself is going to suck me dry like a vampire. Those are the real lessons of survival. What they teach you is a myth. Partly because women are listening. And women tend to need fantasies and myths. Especially from men!

And the biggest, most prevalent myth is that she's going to find that "knight in shining armor," one man who will stick with her for richer, for poorer, in sickness and in health, till death do you part. He's going to "keep" you in the style to which you've become accustomed, says the marriage oath.

\*     \*     \*

A man is called a "catch," because he's trying to run away! There is no equivalent term for women. Women say, "I'm going to get my claws into that man. He's such a catch." These aren't my words. They are the clichés of society.

> **A man is called a "catch," because he's trying to run away!**

Men don't talk like that. We want your companionship, and then we want you to go away and leave us alone to (fill in the blank). In truth, when men want to get together to do guy things (go bowling, play baseball and even go to war), unless there's a sexual element, women get in the way. Ouch, I'm going to get mail. Nonetheless, it's the truth. Ladies, turn to the guy next to you and ask him.

Above and beyond love, sex and marriage (not necessarily the same thing, by the way), this is what it really boils down to: Man is interested in ambition, sex, power and money. He's going to go for it. He has no choice. He can't decide to "stay at home and take care of the kids." It's unacceptable in almost every culture in the world for the man to stay at home and prepare dinner for his hard-working wife. He must work. He must succeed. And, if he knows what's good for him, he must bring home the bacon—to her!! When you really get down to it, things haven't changed all that much from the caveman days. He goes hunting. Risks his life, kills something and brings it home to her. She dines and then he can have some sex.

Today he must first take her out to dinner, before there can be any talk of sex. Men have never understood why, if we've come so far from our primordial past, men and women simply can't have sex together without food or gifts as a prerequisite. Nonetheless, food and gifts ARE a prerequisite. Ask any girl. Ask any guy.

There are a lot of modern, 21st century minded women who have decided to break the rules and make their own fortunes. I applaud them. That way, the ladies might not come after his money when the marriage dissolves (and statistics tell us it will dissolve)...or depend on his money for everything during the marriage, for that matter.

The modern woman who has made her own fortune and doesn't need the man's earning power still depends on the man for some basic things. Biology, at the end of the day, will make its own demands. A man and a woman are in bed together. There's a noise downstairs. She will nudge him and expect him to go down there and risk his life to protect hers.

And even if she's got a .357 Magnum and can take care of business herself, when she goes to see the movie *Love Story* (she has somehow gotten him to go with her—although let's be honest here, he would have just as soon borrowed her .357, put it in his oral cavity and squeezed the trigger rather than go to see this movie)—she expects him to cry at the sensitive parts with her.

She wants a man to be in touch with his feminine side. But, she doesn't have to be in touch with her masculine side, we note! Nonetheless, she wants her man to be able to cry. BUT NOT BEFORE SHE CRIES! If he cries too early he's a wimp, a mama's boy, or gay. If he doesn't cry at all, he's insensitive. If he cries after an appropriate lapse of time, and only *after* she starts crying, then he's a sensitive, caring man.

Now you know why men wanna kill themselves.

# TWO PERFECT DAYS

## The perfect day for her

| | |
|---|---|
| 8:15A.M. | Wake up to hugs and kisses. |
| 8:30A.M. | Weigh in five pounds lighter than yesterday. |
| 8:45A.M. | Breakfast in bed: freshly-squeezed orange juice and croissants. Open presents: expensive jewelry chosen by thoughtful partner. |
| 9:15A.M. | Soothing hot bath with frangipani bath oil. |
| 10:00A.M. | Light workout at club with handsome, funny personal trainer. |
| 10:30A.M. | Facial, manicure, shampoo, blow-dry. |
| 12noon | Lunch with best friend at fashionable outdoor cafe. |
| 12:45P.M. | Catch sight of husband's/boyfriend's ex and notice she has gained twenty pounds |
| 1:00P.M. | Shopping with friends, unlimited credit. |
| 3:00P.M. | Nap. |
| 4:00P.M. | Three dozen roses delivered by florist; card is from secret admirer. |
| 4:15P.M. | Light workout at club, followed by massage from strong but gentle hunk who says he rarely gets to work on such a perfect body. |
| 5:30P.M. | Choose outfit from expensive designer wardrobe: parade before full-length mirror. |
| 7:30P.M. | Candlelit dinner for two followed by dancing, with compliments received by other diners/dancers. |
| 10:00P.M. | Hot shower (alone). |
| 10.50P.M. | Carried to bed (freshly ironed, new, crisp white linen). |
| 11:00P.M. | Pillow talk, light touching and cuddling. |
| 11:15P.M. | Fall asleep in his big strong arms. |

# The perfect day for him

6:00A.M.   Alarm.

6:15A.M.   Blow job.

6:30A.M.   Massive satisfying dump while reading sports section.

7:00A.M.   Breakfast: steak and eggs, coffee and toast, cooked and served by naked buxom wench who bends over a lot showing her growler.

7:30A.M.   Limo arrives.

7:45A.M.   Several beers en route to airport.

9:15A.M.   Flight in personal Learjet.

9:30A.M.   Limo to Mirage Resort Golf Club (blow job enroute).

9:45A.M.   Play front nine, two under.

11:45A.M.   Lunch: hamburger, fries and coke, three beers and a bottle of Dom Perignon.

12:15P.M.   Blow job.

12:30P.M.   Play back nine holes of golf course, four under.

2:15P.M.   Limo back to airport (several bourbons).

2:30P.M.   Fly to deserted fishing hole.

3:30P.M.   Late afternoon fishing expedition with all-female crew, all nude, who frequently bend over a lot displaying growlers.

4:30P.M.   Catch world record Marlin (1,234 pounds) on light tackle.

5:00P.M.   Fly home; massage and hand job by naked Elle McPherson (bending over...naturally).

6:45P.M.   Shit, shower and shave.

7:00P.M.   Watch news: Michael Jackson assassinated; porn legalized.

7:30P.M.   Dinner: lobster appetizers, Dom Perignon (1953), big juicy steak followed by ice-cream served on a big pair of tits.

9:00P.M.   Napoleon Brandy and Cuban cigar in front of wall-size TV as you watch your favorite football team win decisive victory.

9:30P.M.   Sex with three women, all with lesbian tendencies... some bending over.

11:00P.M.   Massage and jacuzzi with tasty pizza snacks and cleansing ale.

11:30P.M.   Nightcap blow job.

11:45P.M.   In bed alone.

11:50P.M.   A twenty-two-second fart that changes note four times and forces dog to leave room.

\*     \*     \*

After a man and a woman make love or have sex (not always the same thing) she does not want him to put *his* head on *her* chest. She wants to put *her* head on *his* chest. She does not care if he feels safe. She wants to feel safe.

Women have penis envy. Save your hate mail. Dig up Freud from his grave and quarrel with him. Not me. Men do not have vagina envy. We're not really all that interested in what it feels like to be born with a vagina. Men do not wonder what it might feel like to be entered. Men don't want to know. (Gay men do, but that's another story.)

Tomboys are little girls who walk, talk, act and dress like boys. These little girls are not gay; these are girls who want to hang with the guys. They may be heterosexual little girls, but they still want to be accepted when the guys get together in their little gangs or play baseball—where little girls, of course, are not welcome. They can't throw the ball, get hurt easily and talk too much (usually about things guys couldn't care less about).

Everything changes once puberty hits. Then the guys are willing to act more on the girls' terms. Why? Sex! The guys stop cursing in front of her, stop talking about baseball and start buying flowers (something they've never done in their lives—except, of course, when they wanted to curry favor from their moms, who are...you guessed it! Big girls).

I'm reminded of that wonderful Mel Gibson movie *What Women Want*. Here's the truth: Men don't care. To be more specific, they're not even curious about the notion. It's not even a blip on their consciousness. Don't worry. I've spoken to the entire population of men in the world, and they say it's OK for me to speak for them. It's about time someone told the truth around here

Women, on the other hand, are constantly trying to figure out men and what makes them tick. "Why won't he call me? Is he seeing another girl? What does all this mean? Where is this relationship leading?" Men don't worry about any of it.

We don't for example, worry about whether we have our mother's thighs. We don't worry about crows feet. We don't have a biological clock, thank God. We are in the here and now. We're hungry; we eat. We're tired; we sleep. What does it all mean? Who cares.

The following is meant to be lighthearted, but there is still some truth in it. See if you agree.

Would man have anything to say to woman if we didn't have sex in common? Most of the men I've spoken to immediately answer "No." Would woman have anything to say to man if we didn't have sex in common? Most of the women I've spoken to immediately answer "Yes." Even if we didn't have anything in common...even if we never had sex...Women will have something to say to men even after the men have died! She will stand over the grave and talk to him until she's blue in the face. Even after he's in the worm-food stage!

Though nature had a grand design, modern technology (created by man) has all but evened the playing field and given women access to all the power they have ever dreamed of having. Women understandably want equal access to power, and nowadays they're getting more of it, because computers don't know the sex of a person and physical prowess doesn't matter all that much anymore. It's all about information. Who has access to it and, most important, who can deliver (or sell) it.

However, no matter how even the playing field has become, the physical world has been and continues to be built by man. Buildings are constructed by men. Women refuse to get out on highways and build roads or get up in the air on scaffolding to build skyscrapers. The truth is that women do want and should have complete and equal access to power, but they don't want equal responsibility. The last thing a woman wants to do is what women do in the Israeli army, which is "time to go to war." Don't kid yourself. The Israeli women don't do all these things because they want to. Their draft is not volunteer. America has a volunteer army. And women don't want to go to Iraq. Who does?

At the end of the day the power of women is completely based on whether she can attract man, biologically speaking. And the power of man has nothing to do with whether he can attract a woman. The power of man is in achieving wealth and "killing things," so we can come back to the cave with a big piece of meat over our shoulder.

Nothing has changed. The ugliest, shortest, baldest guy with the biggest wad of Rupert Murdoch bills in his wallet will attract gorgeous women. And the oldest hag with the biggest wad of bills in her purse will attract nothing! It's tough. Who says we're talking about fair here?

I stand by my words. They're true.

\*     \*     \*

Why do men die younger than their wives? Because they want to. (And because it says on the tombstone above them, "Rest In Peace.") This is just a joke, so relax.

I'm not here to give advice to the lovelorn. I'm not here to tell you what to believe in or what not to believe in. The things I say (and I'll keep reminding you along the way) will shoot big holes through the myths of society and are not necessarily meant to make you happier, but simply to keep more money in your pockets. Then it's up to you to decide what you want to do with it. Give the money to your wife, give it to the government, but if you don't *have* any money you can't give anybody anything.

The prevailing American notion is of a monogamous relationship. When that relationship goes sour—and statistics tell us it

will—the woman is usually paid money: alimony. There are exceptions. Sometimes she pays him. But exceptions don't change the
rule very much. Men still make more money than women, and men
pay alimony. In India marriages are arranged. You never even meet
your wife before the ceremony. You do not marry for love. You "buy
a wife." In the Arab world you buy as many as four wives. Now
remember, in Western culture, it says you promise to keep her in
sickness and in health. *She* doesn't promise to keep *him* in sickness
and in health. He "supports" or "buys" her...don't kid yourself.

And we, in Western culture think, "How primitive, how archaic,"
that people in other societies are willing to pay money to buy a wife
or two. A dowry. I may actually agree with you. The idea of companionship, love and everything else still revolves around money.
We think that Arabs or Indians (from India) have quaint notions
because the husband and wife never even meet until the wedding
day. In Western culture we ask, What about love? It's a good question, but I'm here to tell you that in the American culture of marriage it specifically states that a man has a monetary responsibility
to the woman he's going to marry. The law of the land today is
even more punitive, because it doesn't say anything in the marriage vows about giving her 50 percent of his gross pre-tax dollars.
Wedding vows don't mention an amount of money. Wedding vows
never even mention you're going to get divorced. You're going to
stay with each other till the day you die. In sickness and in health,
for richer or for poorer—even when he's poor, he's going to support
her. That's what it says. During their marriage, not only is he going
to feed, support her and clothe her, but after they get divorced he's
going to give her *even more money*.

In America's case, this is a remnant of the Puritan ethic, which
means if you're not a Puritan you're going to be tortured to death.
What may have worked for the Puritans is probably a very bad idea
for men in the 21st century. It's a great idea for women in the 21st

century. Any philosophy that goes back in time far enough will wind up being unworkable and completely unfair to women in the 21st century. As an example, any woman who wants to make sure it's a monogamous relationship need only look at the Old Testament, where she's just one of a flock, one of many wives. And God said "It's OK. Not a problem."

And it wasn't just the Jews who had multiple wives. In the days of Mohammed and Islam (which came thousands of years later); and the Egyptians and the pagans...lots of wives.

Today men propose marriage to women here in America all the time. This is the same impulse that leads them to beer bashes and drinking too much and driving too fast and not being careful or thoughtful about life. Because if men were completely honest with themselves they would admit privately to the woman they love as they're walking down the aisle (with the rice being thrown, having just told her that he wanted to spend the rest of his life with her) that they don't really believe it. Even as a man is walking back down the aisle from the ceremony, when he sees the bride's girl-friend has a set of double-Ds he's going to look at them. Not because he doesn't love his wife, but because biology dictates that he is visually attracted to that sight. Unconsciously, even though he'll prevent that thought from coming up, he's going to want to have sex with a woman he's never met, whose name he never bothered to learn, just because she has a set of double-Ds.

The oldest, ugliest guy still wants the youngest, prettiest woman, because biology dictates. The thing that makes young women attractive is not necessarily any reason other than because biology makes them able to bear children. "Prettier" means "younger" for women. Men physically stay the same longer. They are able to remain the physical partners women aspire to much later in their lives. It's all about bearing children. That's what makes people appealing.

A woman's appeal is all about breasts and childbearing hips. Only very recently have skinny women—who are barely female, have no breasts and hips and resemble twelve-year-old boys—come into fashion. But that look was created by gay men. If Kate Moss walked down the street do you think she'd stop traffic? No. If Pam Anderson walked down the street, would she stop traffic? Yes! Not because men are necessarily so attracted to her, but because parts of her are "displayed" and "offered." It has been proven over and over again that a woman with large breasts will stop traffic. Men will whistle and howl and otherwise make complete spectacles of themselves. Flat-chested women don't have that effect. Men won't even look twice.

And men with erections in their pants make women turn around and look, even though they'll try not to. If it doesn't look like he has a basket, you're not going to look down there. It's the visual stimulus. Colors and breasts and hips. Bras are invented for what, for comfort? Bras were invented to make breasts look bigger, so men will look. They're padded and they have water and there are WonderBras that lift and separate. The phrase "T&A" stands for "tits and ass." That's what it's all about. Look at any cover of *Playboy*. Is the woman as attractive with small or no breasts? Of course not. Is she more attractive to men if her breasts are bigger? Absolutely. Going all the way back to the first pieces of erotic clay art found in caves. It's never been any different. And there's no reason for breasts to be big at all. Biologically, that is. Because women with very small breasts or flat chests produce just as much milk in their milk ducts as big-breasted women. It is purely nature's way of attracting men. Breasts have gotten bigger and bigger because men are so attracted to them as a visual stimulus—no other reason.

At a party I hosted recently every single female there had on her perfume, her high heels, her make-up, push-up bra, hairdo, the loud colors...all that stuff. That's where her power lies...in attracting men. Whether she does anything with him or not is another story. The men maybe put on cologne. They might change into a nicer jacket. But other than that they don't try to alter their image. They don't tend to change their hair color or wear false eyelashes—by and large, they don't *have* to.

*   *   *

The reason sexuality is so different between men and women is that a woman's most sensitive point on her body is completely hidden. It takes a long time to get to the button that sends her up to the third floor—*"I'm coming!"* Imagine you're a man. Your most sensitive part brushes against your pants leg every time you take a step forward. Women keep saying to men, "Why can't you control yourself?" There's a physical reason why they can't! Not only are billions of sperm trying to get out, if he doesn't physically let them out by ejaculating in the form of intercourse or by manipulating himself, they will explode like a volcano anyway. If he doesn't, he'll dream about it. Think about it.

> So the old phrase "A man thinks with his dick" is correct. We have enough blood in our system for one head, probably not enough for two.

And so the old phrase "A man thinks with his dick" is correct. We have enough blood in our system for one head, probably not enough for two. And when the other head thinks, there's a financial price to be paid. This is the real point about love for men—it's completely different for women. He may want to have a family and a house and children and so on, but he's not going to want to curtail his attraction and accessibility to other females. There is no other reason I can think of why divorce is so high in Western culture. It's because men want to have sex with other women. He's not cheating *biologically*; he's doing *exactly* what biology dictates. He's cheating biology of its prime directive—the urge to merge—if he *doesn't* go after other women.

The idea of "cheating" is based on a woman's notions. Her man is cheating the woman of her sole access to that man. To her exclusive use of his sexual appendage. But more specifically he's cheating her of his time, which is the threat that he may leave her and go to another woman, whom he'll keep and give money to and so on. Alienation of affection is now a legal recourse. A woman can go to the courts and say, "This woman had a relationship with my husband and took away the money that I would normally have from this guy." This is the law of the land. It is a man's responsibility to realize that once he gets married, even though God has given him two balls, one is now hers.

The worst thing a man can do, financially and biologically speaking, is to get married. Because when his body is making sperm, which is twenty-four hours a day, it produces billions and billions. They're not all lined up directed at one woman. They explode out like pollen from a tree, in every single direction. What women want is what I would want if I were a woman: to undermine the ability of every other woman to have access to this man and his abilities to make money. Money is Social Security for a woman.

Men who go to bars sooner or later will want to go get some girls. As soon as a man takes a step forward the head of his appendage will remind him. It rubs up against his pants and says, "Hey! What about me!" twenty-four hours a day, even in your sleep. Men can wake up in the middle of the night with a "peepee-tepee." Something is standing straight up, all on its own. "Can't you control yourself?" women demand. The answer is "no."

You will know when we think you're cute, because "he's" going to stand at attention, even if we don't want "him" to.

As little boys we can't make him go away. In class when a teacher has big perky breasts, the little ten- and twelve-year-old boys get rock hard. They're afraid to stand up at the end of class, because they can't control their penis. They can't make it go away. And women know this, but refuse to acknowledge it. "Control yourself." But you don't want us to control ourselves with you. You just want us to control ourselves around *other women*. Unfortunately, it's the antithesis of what biology has dictated for men. Therein lies the big problem.

> The only thing **wrong** with marriage is that one of the two people getting married **is a man.** He will tend to stray. She will tend not to. She only makes one or two eggs; he makes billions of sperm. The defense rests, your honor. Next case.

This whole system has worked for women for a long time. It's been a disaster for men. Because men keep getting tortured for their attraction to other women. And when they act on this attraction, divorce is the result. It doesn't reflect all the liaisons that woman have forgiven men for and decided not to file for divorce. If I had to take a guess, I'd say that about 80 or 90 percent of men cheat. There was a poll on CNN once—something like 70 percent of men admitted to having extramarital affairs. What about the ones who *weren't* willing to admit it? Could the true figure be 90 percent or more? Yes. Because biology says you're supposed to.

And men should fight this urge— *financially*. Men and women can decide to get married or not to get married. There are two or three notions that they both have to deal with. For men, they're very clear. For women, they're fighting an uphill battle, and they're willing to be paid for the privilege of fighting that battle. The only thing wrong with marriage is that one of the two people getting married is a man. He will tend to stray. She will tend not to. She only makes one or two eggs; he makes billions of sperm. The defense rests, your honor. Next case.

*　　*　　*

A man makes, by and large, much more money than a woman does. And even if he doesn't make a lot more money than she does, if they get divorced and he gives her half at the highest tax rate, she can still go on and make money at her job, win lotteries, what have you, and it doesn't knock down the price of her half. She gets to keep the half *and* the money she makes at work.

Right, wrong, fair, unfair...that's not what this is all about. A man's standard of living goes up after a divorce because he doesn't have to pay for two people all the time. When he goes to dinner he's not paying for both. Of course his standard of living goes up! Not to mention that he can work longer hours without hearing the phrase "You love your job more than me." In marriages men tend to be less ambitious, because you need time for your family.

How many clichés have you heard about fathers who weren't there for their children? Many. But you don't hear it about mothers. There's a biological reason for that. The tendency is that—and I'm painting with wide strokes here—men love their children. But if that's all we had, I have a feeling the suicide rate among men would go up. Because man's directive is to *do* something. We cannot subsist only by being there and nurturing and being loved in return. It doesn't work. We're built differently. We have larger muscles—for

# How To Shower Like A Woman

Take off clothing and place in sectioned laundry basket according to lights, darks, whites, manmade or natural. Walk to shower wearing long dressing gown. If husband/boyfriend is seen along the way, cover up any exposed flesh and rush to bathroom.

Examine womanly physique in the mirror and stick out belly. Complain and whine about getting fat. Get in shower. Look for face cloth, arm cloth, loin cloth, long loofah, wide loofah and pumice stone. Wash hair once with cucumber shampoo with eighty-three added vitamins.

Wash hair again, then apply cucumber conditioner with enhanced natural crocus oil. Leave on hair for fifteen minutes. Wash face with crushed apricot facial scrub for ten minutes until red and raw. Wash entire rest of body with ginger-nut and apricot body wash. Rinse conditioner from hair, taking at least fifteen minutes to make sure it's all off.

Shave armpits and legs. Consider shaving bikini area but decide to get it waxed instead. Scream loudly when husband/boyfriend flushes toilet and water loses pressure and turns cold. Turn off shower. Squeegee all wet surfaces in shower. Get out of shower. Dry off with towel the size of a small African nation. Wrap hair in super-absorbent second towel. Check entire body for remotest signs of spots. Attack with nails-tweezers (if you can find any). Return to bedroom wearing long dressing gown and towel on head. If husband/boyfriend sees you, cover up any exposed areas then rush to bedroom to spend an hour and a half getting dressed.

# How To Shower Like A Man

Take off clothes while sitting on bed and leave them in a pile. Walk naked to bathroom. If seen by wife/girlfriend, shake willy at her and shout, "Wa-hey!" Look in mirror and suck in gut to see manly physique. Admire size of willy in mirror and scratch balls. Get in shower. Don't bother to look for washcloth—don't need one. Wash face. Wash armpits. Laugh at how loud farts sound in the shower. Wash balls and surrounding area. Wash arse, leaving hair on the soap. Shampoo hair but do not use conditioner. Make Mohican hairstyle with shampoo. Pull back curtain to see self in mirror. Piss in shower.

Rinse off and get out of shower. Fail to notice water on floor caused by shower curtain being outside bath for entire showering time. Partially dry off. Look at self in mirror, flex muscles and admire size of willy again.

Leave shower curtain open and wet bath mat on floor. Leave on bathroom light and fan. Return to bedroom with towel around waist, leaving wet footprints on carpets. If you pass wife/girlfriend, pull off towel, grab willy, go "Yeah, baby" and thrust pelvis at her. Put on yesterday's clothes.

YEAH, BABY

what? To hold and cuddle a baby in our arms? Why are we so much bigger than women are if we're meant to stay home? We're meant to build the world. Women are deluding themselves to think otherwise.

But for women it's financially beneficial to believe in their own myth, because the more you argue "No, we're exactly the same," the more money you'll get. Which is why everything I say is not an even-handed idea. It is a wake-up call to all men, that if they don't want to pay anyone money for companionship, don't get married. Because the biggest contributing factor to divorce is marriage. If you don't want to pay the price of divorce, don't get married. If you're willing to pay the price of divorce, or living together with a woman for more than two years, the only recourse you have is to have some legal protection. Not a pre-nup, because a pre-nup by definition supposes you're getting "nupped."

Which means there's going to be half men and half women on the jury in a divorce case, and in a trial by jury a woman on the stand can always cry. When that happens the trial is over for the man. When a husband is put on the stand he can't use that tool. He can't cry. "She's taking all my money that I worked so hard for!" It just doesn't work. He will lose. The jury and the judge and everyone else have to go home to a wife. Some of the men will vote with the woman, and the husband is fucked, and I don't mean the way he wants to be.

> ## Because the biggest contributing factor to divorce is marriage. If you don't want to pay the price of divorce, don't get married.

I realize that this book will greatly upset women and be a kick-in-the-butt wake-up call to men. It's easy for men to buck social convention—they want to do and tend to do what comes naturally, which is chase after skirt. It's harder for women, because what women have been fighting is the uphill battle. Women are fighting biology's prime directive, which is that man has a bigger chance of improving the gene pool the more women he impregnates. That is nature talking. Women are saying no matter what nature tells man to do, I want to be the only one! The only woman he impregnates. It's a problem for women, not for men.

Dumb men will always get married. So will smart women. There is a phrase, a cliché perhaps, "old maid." There is no male equivalent. If a man never gets married and never has children nobody cares. If a woman never gets married and never has children, there is a societal stigma, mostly from women. In point of fact, single men prefer to go with women who don't have children. They don't want to deal with children at home. Because they want to be left alone. They don't want the responsibility. They want to come and play and then be left alone to pursue their ambitions. It is less attractive to men when a woman walks up, no matter how sexy she is, if she has a child. Because there are financial repercussions.

> **Dumb men will always get married. So will smart women.**

\*     \*     \*

The following is food for thought. Please don't get upset! A prostitute will at least have the honesty and integrity of "full disclosure." Before any kind of physical activity happens, she will tell you how much money she wants for the act! Your wife-to-be will tell you nothing. She will never tell you that as your wife she expects you to put a roof over her head, buy her clothing, food and so on. This is understood and expected by a woman. Ignorance of the law is no excuse. Men don't necessarily think about it. Women do!

> **A prostitute will at least have the honesty and integrity of "full disclosure." _Before_ any kind of physical activity happens, she will tell you how much money she wants for the act!**

My suggestion to all couples is before you start a relationship, certainly before you enter into a two-year cohabitation: Get individual counsel and soberly, above and beyond love and all the other matters of the heart, simply deal with the matters of the three-dimensional world in which we live. That means money. Talk about contingencies and a sunset clause. Talk about what happens _if_...Talk about everything before. It's called full disclosure. Don't jump into the deep end of the pool, especially emotionally, if you don't know how deep the financial pool is. If you're not sure you can swim, don't jump.

Take the scenario of a couple who gets married right out of college. The wife works and pays the rent and all the other bills while her husband goes through medical school. This goes on for years as he graduates from school, does his residency, sets up a practice and so on. When they split up—and statistically, they *will* split up—should she get half? Yes, absolutely. But on the flip side, if *he* supported *her* for years while she stayed at home, should *he* get half of hers? He supported her—fed her, clothed her, paid for her medical care, she never had to work. Think about it.

Your kids (after the age of five) spend most of the day in school. Should teachers get a percentage of your gross dollars, since they educate your kids, watch out for them, and spend the most amount of time with them? Who loves them more? Mom and Dad. But who teaches them more? Teachers! Should *they* get half? If you think so, pay them! What's the price for giving birth? Discuss it...*together* ...*before!!*

The point I'm trying to make is that any scenario—a relationship, marriage, boyfriend, girlfriend—anything that impacts one day more than two years becomes a *legally binding arrangement.* You may as well be married, because the same rules apply. Both men and women owe it to themselves to be completely upfront. She should say, "Here's what I want," and make a wish list. He should say, "Here's what I want," and make a wish list. If both parties can't agree beforehand, don't start the relationship. Or at least don't live together for one day longer than two years.

Now, as an aside to all women: I urge you to keep on doing what you're doing—don't tell him a single thing until you get married—because once you get married and then divorced, it's going to be the single biggest financial windfall you will ever have in your life, and you'll be able to keep all the money you make at your jobs as well. Not to mention the new husband(s) you will eventually divorce and take fifty percent from.

For men: While you're dating, if she wants to go to dinner, the rules of society say you're going to pay. If you're going to live together, by and large you'll pay the rent. If she wants to go buy something, you will pay for it. If you're going on a vacation trip, you'll pay for it. If there are going to be anniversary gifts (jewelry), you're buying. If she gets sick you'll pay the medical bills. And once you finally get divorced and the proceedings are over, you will pay her fifty percent. And once she gets all the money, she can also go out and make a living, keep your alimony and her salary as well.

If you don't make sure to speak up before the fact, you will pay the single largest bill of your entire life. To one person. Here's the shocking thing: it's not going to be to the person who gave you life itself, your mother. You will pay somebody you met after you grew up more than your mother, who gave you birth, sustenance, blood and milk. Your mother won't even get a few phone calls a week. She'll complain about it, but there are no real repercussions. But if you don't call your wife often enough you'll get hell.

*   *   *

Both men and women want to feel safe with each other. Safe to men means "Don't steal my money." Safe to women means "I want financial security."

Perhaps the only way women can understand this concept is by comparing rape and lovemaking. To someone from another galaxy, the difference might be perplexing. Rape and lovemaking look very similar. The difference is choice. Both usually involve penetration. The difference is one is given wholeheartedly; the other is taken brutally. Rape in my world would be *her* hand in *my* pocket. If it's OK with me and given with all my heart, she can take as much as she wants. If it's without my consent, she can't have a penny. I may truly want to give her every dime I have, but if she tries to steal a penny from me, I will spend every nickel I have to fight her, simply for the principle of it.

Women don't want to be raped. Neither do men.

If men and women don't want the government, courts or soci-

In 1972, Paul and I had decided to disband a group called Wicked Lester. It consisted of Brooke Ostrander (keyboards), Tony Zarella (drums), Stephen Coronel (guitar), Paul and myself. We had succeeded in getting Epic Records to give us a recording contract. But all was not well. There was a gnawing feeling that this was not the band that would go the distance.

Paul and I told the other members we intended to move on without them. The response, at least from Tony, our drummer, was that he had a contract to be in the band and he planned to honor it—a nice way of saying, you can't fire me. So Paul and I did the next best thing: We quit.

We had a loft at 10 East 23rd street we rehearsed in. It cost $200 a month. Paul and I shared the rent after Lester disbanded, and Paul worked at his cab-driving job. He liked working nights so he could sleep during the days. But we rehearsed at night, so it made driving a cab difficult and limited.

The loft was a rat-infested firetrap, with no windows and only one door at the end of the room. The walls were soon covered by discarded egg crates, which we got from supermarkets. Unfortunately, some of the eggs had been crushed, so there was egg residue on some of them. Of course, as soon as the lights went out, a cockroach stampede ensued in the dark. Unfortunately for me, because I worked in the daytime at the Puerto Rican Interagency Council in uptown Manhattan, I didn't have enough time to go to my mother's house in Queens, change and then come to rehearsals at night in Manhattan. I was forced to move my bed into the loft and often spent nights there. I also worked as a checkout guy at a local deli, so I could earn additional money and eat as much as I wanted for free. I often brought my dinners to the loft. That didn't help the roach problem, either.

Without the songwriters and singers in the band, Epic soon dropped Wicked Lester.

Paul and I started writing new songs and soon found a "sound." We had only to find a drummer, we thought, to make the sound come alive. The story has been told over and over again, but in short order, due to an ad in Rolling Stone, we found Peter Criscuola (Peter Criss), who became our drummer. We tried playing as a trio and actually applied a primitive form of

what was to become our KISS make-up. It looked more like Mime make-up (the French art form).

We invited Epic Records vice president Don Ellis down to our loft to show him that although Wicked Lester had changed, we were ready with the new lineup—as a trio—and new songs to honor the contract. Needless to say, after Peter's drunk brother, who was in attendance with a few invited guests, threw up on him, Ellis stormed out muttering something like "I'll call you."

So, here we were. A new band. Without a name. Without a record contract.

We decided we needed a lead guitarist, and after many bizarre auditions, we took in Paul "Ace" Frehley. It was a volatile mixture. But they say everything is chemistry. Either you have it or you don't. We had it.

I called around town to try to find us a club that would book us. The answer was usually a resounding "no" when they found out we didn't do cover versions of the day's disco hits. But one club in Sunnyside, Queens called Popcorn decided to let us play three days in a row, on their slow nights—Tuesday, Wednesday and Thursday—for $35 a night and a percentage of the door. We didn't care how little we were getting paid. We just wanted to play. We were still Wicked Lester.

By the time the club date came, we had become KISS. Ace hand-drew the original KISS logo on a blown-up picture of Wicked Lester (although we didn't wear make-up in the photo), and Paul soon drew the KISS logo that was to be used as the official logo—to this day. We had a primitive form of our KISS make-up, though we didn't have the whiteface on. We simply drew black designs around our eyes. Paul wore no make-up designs at all. He just wore some rouge on his cheeks. Ditto for Ace. Peter wore some make-up designs around his eyes. And I had the first version of my "bat" design.

In the audience was Jan, my then-girlfriend, a friend of hers and Lydia Criss, Peter's then-wife. That was the entire audience. Three people!!!

Here we are in never-before-seen photos playing our hearts out as if we were onstage at Madison Square Garden—to three people.

KISS is born!!!

In 1980, KISS visited Australia for the first time. The band had conquered America and Japan in the 70s, and we had survived an imminent breakup. Our drummer Peter Criss left the band, and new drummer Eric Carr joined us on his first-ever tour. Neither he nor the band knew what to expect.

The people were beautiful, the weather was perfect and we were trapped in a cage of our own making. We had created this make-up-wearing band, and the press photographers were out in full force trying to get a shot of us without our make-up on. We usually holed up in our hotel rooms as helicopters with telescopic lenses hovered just outside our windows. When we wanted to venture out in daylight, we would don disguises, like wearing our own version of famed nineteenth-century Aussie bandit Ned Kelly's helmet. Sometimes we rented a boat, filled it with Aussie girls and headed out into Sydney harbor to have an uninterrupted party. At night we would rent out an entire club and fill it with friends and, of course, girls. Lots of them.

The popularity of the band in Australia is best described this way: One in every fourteen Australians had either KISS tickets or albums. These photos show the crowd that showed up at Sydney Town Hall, where the Mayor of the city held court and declared an official welcome to the band.

The photos speak for themselves.

# MY DAD THE ROCK STAR

EXCLUSIVE

JANUARY, 2001

**TRUE LIFE STORY:**
REBEL WITHOUT A
NOSE-RING

Willy or won't he?
– get to know
the *real*
Willy Zilla

CREATED BY
Gene Simmons

SERIES BIBLE
written by
Tim Burns
& Dale Schott

SNEAK PEEK
INSIDE THE
SKUNK CAVE

7 42709 10020 8

# JUST ONE OF THE GUYS

*I never wanted kids. I found myself saying that ever since I can remember. I also never wanted to get married, for a number of reasons. You could walk out on a marriage (although it would be expensive), but how does one walk out on kids? I believe I never wanted kids purely out of fear.*

*And yet I not only had a kid, I had two of them. I couldn't have been more wrong about my fears. My son and daughter are the single greatest joy I have ever known. I found myself writing little stories about Nick and Sophie. I drew little doodles for them. I made up stories to put them to sleep.*

*And when I talked about them to people, more than one person said it sounded like a situation comedy.*

*Because my son in particular tries very hard to fit in and be "just one of the guys," I found his life strangely fascinating. When I met up with Toper Taylor, who was president of Nelvana, a cartoon production company, we tossed around the idea of a KISS cartoon show at first. But we couldn't come to agree on the deal points. I was not going to let them or anyone else have access to KISS for pennies, when I knew it was worth dollars.*

*As we threw around ideas I started talking about my relationship with my son. Out of that came* My Dad, The Rock Star. *The premise of the cartoon show was that a family moves to Middle America. The young boy of the family (age twelve) goes to school and tries to fit in. He experiences his first kiss. He has friends. But when his friends come over to his house and knock on the front door, the person who answers has fire coming out of his ass and a talking cod-piece. The boy also has an older sister whose main purpose in life is to torture him. His mother is a survivor of the hippie movement. His pet is a seven-foot-long Komodo dragon who wears shades, constantly watches TV and talks to himself.*

*The show began production on more than one occasion, and then stopped. It has been stop and go for years. It is currently in the "stop" part of the process while Nelvana re-organizes. It will soon begin the "go" cycle. Cartoons take years to see the light of day. This one is no different.*

# DETROIT
# ROCK CITY

As a Producer on our film Detroit Rock City I initially thought my "duties" would be to develop the material, liase with the studio, consult with our director and numerous other jobs. After the movie was delivered to the studio, I realized that the work had just begun. The marketing department started having meetings with studio heads Bob Shaye and Mike De Luca. I would sit in these meetings with my co-producers. Everyone was trying to figure out whether the movie should be directed right down the middle at the KISS fan, or whether it should be marketed more as a general comedy film. If the artwork for the posters skewed too "male" would it turn off the females? If it came off too "light" would it turn off the males? If it was too "KISS" would the rest of the world care? If it didn't mention KISS at all, would KISS fans turn away?

The posters had a lot to do with the public's perception of the movie. The marketing department came in with literally fifty different posters. I know—I have them all. Some of them were far too busy. A few of them hit the mark. But the actors in our film were mostly unknown to the masses, so featuring four unknown faces on a poster didn't make a lot of sense.

I liked one of the sample posters that featured a hand signal. It was a variation of the hand signal I originated. My hand signal—commonly referred to as the "heavy metal" hand signal—came from Steve Ditko's comic book, Dr. Strange. After I started doing it in photos and nine live concerts, everyone followed suit. It has now become a cliché. People have stopped doing it. I still do it. It's my signal, after all.

I liked the idea of using the hand signal on the poster only because it seemed to "epitomize" an era—the 70s. I thought it would become memorable. I pushed for it. Our director Adam Rifkin had another idea. He was a fan of Stanley Kramer's It's A Mad, Mad Mad, Mad World, a comedy that became the template for funny chase movies. The movie poster featured everyone in the cast. Needless to say, the Mad World cast included over twenty comedians. So Rifkin paid to have his version of the poster done. Everyone was depicted in the poster. Producers were in it. Shannon Tweed was in it. I was in it. Everyone loved it.

So we decided to use that poster for our film. And because of that, I'm sorry to say, the original art of the poster proudly sits in Adam's house, instead of mine.

The complete weekly entertainment guide
July 17–24, 1996  Issue No. 43  $1.95

# TimeOut
## New Yor

**Fore play**
Mini golf for
big people

**Websites of
champions**
The Olympics
compete online

**Hard schlock
cafés**
Scoping out the
city's theme
shops and
restaurants

## KISS
# THIS!

**Trading licks backstage
with the '70s gods of thunder**

Plus: the Kiss walking tour?!?
**The band recalls its NYC haunts**

# THE BEST DOCTOR FOR YOUR KIDS

MAY 7, 2001

# NEW YORK

## Mack Is Back

Grown up at 20, with a new play on Broadway, **Macaulay Culkin** tells the story of his lost childhood. By Ariel Levy

**Plus**

**Cramer: How to Get Back Into Tech Stocks Now**

$2.99 (CANADA $3.99)

0 74820 08183 9

19>

NEWYORKMAG.COM

# LA WEEKLY

FREE

# Wild Thing?

Live music, dead fish and Cleveland's rock repository

BY GREG BURK

Sunday News

Oct. 16, 1977

magazine

## Paddleball boom!

The city game
that's off the wall

How to get out of debt

Blouses:
The frill is back

GRAND·ILLUSION

By 2001, I began to take a serious look at re-entering motion picture and television production. I started to look at mounting a KISS Broadway play. So far, it hasn't happened. But one thing leads to another, and along the way I got a phone call from a Scott Steindorff, who was interested in meeting to talk about some projects he had.

We met and I got involved in close to ten different projects with him. One of them is a movie about to start shooting. I found out his background was in real estate. He had also been a sportsman and had written the Las Vegas stage show EFX (which first starred Tommy Tune and then Rick Springfield and has been running for close to a decade). He was interested in getting involved in a new Vegas show and wanted me to join him.

At first we came up with a Las Vegas club, or room, where multi-media events would be taking place around you in a very private area. We wanted to call it the Gene Simmons Theater. Not a great title. But I liked the first part of it.

From that we segued into an original idea—how about a show based around Studio 54, I offered. How about the idea that, at its zenith, 54 was "the" place to be. Everyone wanted to get in. Very few people did. The Gate Keeper would be the "arbiter" of who was cool and who was not. So we came up with a storyline about a loser who wanted to win. And a lonely girl who wanted to belong. And, of course, about a powerful and attractive man (me) who might give them what they wanted. For a price.

I called it "Grand Illusion"—it was to be the name of the club. Reality existed outside the club. Inside the club, anything was possible. Its only limitations were your imagination. Once inside the club, you could have anything you wanted. But was it real?

We sold the idea to one of the biggest Vegas hotels. We negotiated (and got) a letter saying that we could "four wall" (or own all the tickets of) the show. That was a coup. But after we did the cost breakdowns, we decided it needed a television component to increase the profit potential three-fold and to minimize financial risk to a bare minimum. We couldn't deliver the television side. Not yet.

But we still have the deal, and time is on our side. And the dark figure seated in the chair? He's still there.

I've always been blessed with this delusional notion I have of myself: I think I'm better-looking than I actually am. What I mean is I'm consciously aware that I'm neither the best-looking nor the worst-looking guy in the world. But I'm also aware that I can walk into any room and walk out with your girlfriend—no matter how good-looking you are.

This has always served me well.

They call it self-esteem. If that's the case, I have lots of it. Or perhaps (again) I'm delusional. But so long as I believe it, it's real to me.

I've heard people say they hate the sound of their own voice. I find that peculiar, because I actually love the sound of my own voice. I've heard actors say they can't watch themselves on-screen because they pick out their own facial tics. Or they don't like the way they enunciate. I love the way I talk. Humble be damned.

I say that elsewhere in this book, but it bears repeating. Being humble is for cowards or very polite people. I'm polite (I can hold my gas with the best of them), but I'm also truthful. About everything. But especially about myself.

All of which leads me to my Australian lecture tour. I was busy writing my book Kiss and Make-Up, and was pleasantly surprised when it became a New York Times bestseller (yes, I know I've mentioned that once or twice). I thought the life of the book would stop after sales stopped. I was wrong.

Because of the book, I started to get offers for speaking engagements. First at UCLA, then at the New Music Convention in Vancouver, and then to the University of Florida. They even gave me money (I love that part).

So when Australia called, by way of a lecture agency that had brought over President Bill Clinton for a series of speeches, I bit. I wasn't sure what they wanted me to talk about. As you can guess by now, I tend to talk (mostly) about myself...a subject I know a lot about. While it's true they were interested in me as a person, they were more curious about how I led my life and my personal choices for happiness. You know the drill by now: No marriage. No one is allowed to dictate where I go, where I've been, and so on. There was also a great deal of attention paid to my peculiar ideas about how one's personal life and business life aren't that different at all. Which is to say, a guy (in particular) would never give anyone he's negotiating a business deal with the chance to own a percentage of his gross, pre-tax dollars...but this same knucklehead will not think twice about standing next to someone he's just met (relatively speaking) and under most circumstances (divorce) that's exactly what will happen.

But "That's love." I'm always being told that. I have no quarrel with love. I just want to know why it's so expensive.

Or why I have to pay for it in the first place.

**LEA**

THE MAGAZINE FOR
MAGAZINE MANAGEMENT
foliomag.com

April 2002 | $8.00

# Folio:

ZIFF DAVIS LOOKS TO
REBOOT THE CRASHED
IT ECONOMY

FILMLESS WORKFLOWS:
ARE YOU READY?

THE USPS' PLAN TO
GET OFF CONGRESS'
HIGH-RISK LIST

## KISS + SELL

GENE SIMMONS VOWS HE'LL PUT THE
CHIC IN *TONGUE*—FASTER, CHEAPER AND BETTER
THAN PUBLISHING'S OTHER STAR PLAYERS

MEDIA CENTRAL
PRIMEDIA PUBLICATION

Folio *magazine is the trade publication of the magazine industry. They ran a cover story on* GENE SIMMONS TONGUE. *Their point of view didn't focus so much on Gene Simmons the entrepreneur, but on the business structure of our magazine and the chances it had in the decidedly unfriendly climate of the current magazine market.*

*My partner Allen Tuller and I decided to be lean and mean. We wouldn't have West Coast offices as such. I simply worked out of my office at home. I have more square footage there then most offices, anyway. We save rent and electricity monies. We also decided not to have "full-time staff." The problem with full-time staff in the United States (in most states, except "Right To Work" states) is that the law demands the employer pay for items that have nothing to do with the work performed.*

*When a plumber comes to fix my plumbing, he only has the right to charge me for the work he's performed. He doesn't expect me to pick up his 401K tax returns. He doesn't expect me to have a separate room for "Day Care," in case he's a she and has children she wants to bring to work with her. He doesn't expect me to have a Pension Fund (in other words, put money away so that when he retires he can have that money, too). He doesn't come in and hit me up for raises. He and I simply agree on a price for his work beforehand. He does what he's paid to do, and then he leaves.*

*Everyone on our magazine is an independent contractor. They work, in essence, on one photo shoot or one article at a time. At the beginning of the assignment, they are hired. At the end of the assignment, their work is no longer required (conceptually).*

*The astonishing thing is that if we had a full-time work force it would be almost impossible to fire anyone, for any reason. The Union could very well challenge the firing, and then you're in court. We want to be able to hire and fire anyone as we see fit. If you do the job, you stay. If you don't, you're gone. No fuss. No muss. No Unions.*

*The quality of our magazine, I like to think, is top-notch. The money is spent in the right places: In the pages and the content. So while excellent magazines like Miramax's* Talk *cost millions to launch (by some estimates over $10 million), our first issue cost just over $50,000. Our circulation is approaching 500,000. That's neck and neck with the most successful magazines out there—for a fraction of the cost.*

*Folio was interested in our business model—the cover says it all: "Gene Simmons vows he'll put the chic in* TONGUE—*faster, cheaper and better than publishing's other star players."*

*But try as I might, I couldn't lose the fellow on my right—that's Allen Tuller sticking out his tongue.*

This tattoo recently done on the body part of a fan is a particular honor for me. While most people know me as the guy who sticks out his tongue, the other "non-make-up" me is every bit as big a part of who I am. And the "moneybag" logo underneath both our faces seems to perfectly fit in between the Jekyll/Hyde duo.

Question is, who came first?

I've always said our fans are the best in the world. Any band would give their left nut to have the kind of loyalty we have. But I usually don't talk about the astonishing amount of talent out there. As proof, I offer this portrait of yours truly done by a fan for a school project.

The detail on the arms, the jacket and even my face are actual song lyrics. See if you can pick them out.

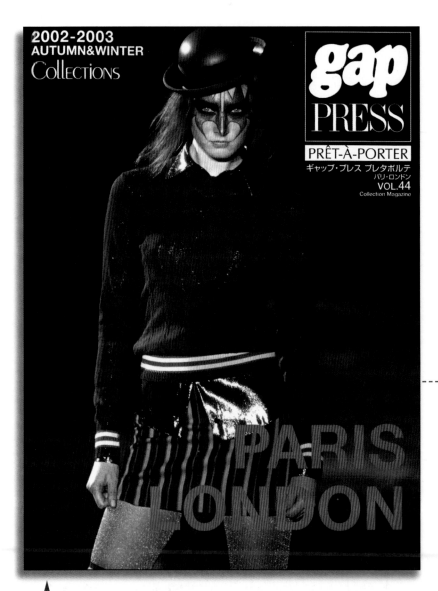

2002-2003
AUTUMN&WINTER
Collections

*gap*
PRESS

PRÊT-À-PORTER
ギャップ・プレス プレタポルテ
パリ・ロンドン
VOL.44
Collection Magazine

PARIS
LONDON

*I always wanted to be in a rock band, but I was never satisfied with being thought of simply as a musician. When we did licensing and merchandising, the emphasis was placed on our faces or facial designs, rather than on the instruments we played. So photos of myself in magazines didn't often show me posing with my bass. Usually, the close-up was of my face.*

*If it works, what you create becomes bigger than itself. When that happens, your creation becomes part of culture.*

*This is a Japanese magazine called Gap Press, featuring the latest fashion trends on the catwalks of Paris 2002-2003. The young lady on the cover is wearing clothing designed by Alexander McQueen.*

*She is wearing make-up designed by Gene Simmons.*

# THE 20 HOTTEST WOMEN IN HISTORY!

## GENE SIMMONS
# Tongue

### SEX ★ STYLE ★ ROCK N' ROLL

you don't know
# JACK!

G-Spot:
## PUT THE X
## IN SEX!

# NIKKI ZIERING
**come on down!**

# TRAVIS TRITT
**tells it like it is**

# ZITO RULES
facing off with Chuck Zito

# NHRA
**hot rods & hot girls**

## GIRLS GONE WILD
EXPOSED!

## SHANNON ELIZABETH
**wild party pix**

the face behind
# THE HULK
marvel mogul unmasked

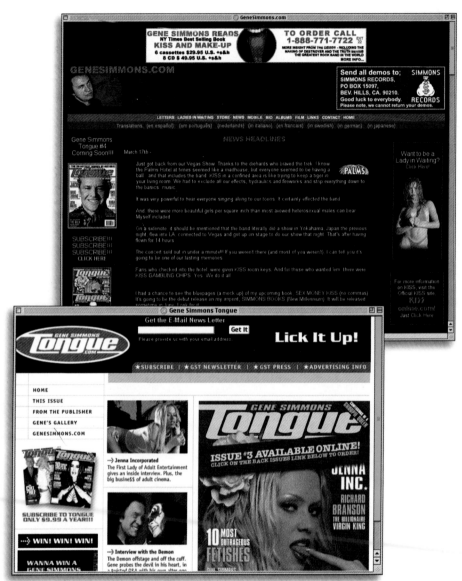

ety deciding for them what the price of intimacy should be, then due diligence and cohabitation agreements are the answer. Perhaps the reason I am devoting so much space to the nature of relationships, and especially their financial repercussions, is because this book is intended to shine a spotlight on things that would otherwise go scurrying back into the dark. It's time to shed some light on fantasy and talk about reality. *Financial* reality. I make no judgments, I make no claims; and you are free to make your own decisions and pay the consequences for your decisions.

There are three basic kinds of agreements that govern living arrangements (check with a lawyer in your state), whether or not you utilize them. *Marriage* is the obvious one, and the most common, with more than 56 million married couples in the United States today (that's 112 million people). The rules of marriage are slightly different in every state. Few couples sign pre-nuptial agreements before they get married, which have their own rules and vary by couple. There are *common-law marriages*, the laws of which are slightly different in every state. And finally, there are *cohabitation agreements*.

I will take this opportunity to remind men: it's to your financial benefit before you fall in love, and before you do anything, whether it's for a lifetime or just a few years, to have full disclosure. Tell her everything: what you're willing to do financially, and what you're not willing to do. Women, on the other hand, should do that only if they are financially foolish. My advice to women is to be as vague as possible, because there's no other way to reap the full financial benefits of divorce. If a man realizes before he gets married what the price of that relationship is going to be, he may very well decide not to get married!

Women benefit when they make sure that a man is dazzled by love and doesn't have enough time to think things through before rushing into marriage. I offer the following: He says to her, "I love you, but before we go further I'd like to discuss what happens in case we ever get divorced. How much money would you like?" Her response might be to avoid the issue, cry and say it's unromantic to talk about it. Men, you better run as fast as your legs can carry you. Because anybody who you're supposed to share your bed and your life with who refuses to talk about *your* money is giving you a harbinger of things to come.

The laws of marriage have nothing to do with love. It's a financial arrangement that usually benefits women. And the poorer the man is, the more a dollar hurts when it leaves his pocket.

*   *   *

Many readers will find all this very disturbing. The reason is that it's the truth, and part of the power women have is that the financial ramifications of relationships to men don't quite get out there. Some of the comments I've gotten about my ideas on marriage are "How can you say anything about marriage until you've experienced it?" I've also never been shot by a gun, but I have a sneaking suspicion I might not like it. The notion that you have to experience something before you can comment on it is only made by fools. One can learn by observing, or learn nothing by experiencing. It may be akin to having your face too close to the mirror: While it's true the mirror shows your reflection, you may also be too close to see anything. Perspective is always the most important thing.

I like the freedom of being able to decide for myself what to do, how hard to work, and how to spend my money without giving it to anyone. I refuse to check with anyone how I should spend my money. That feeling is indescribable. Men, who usually have to check with someone; and women, who have to check with a man on how they can spend their money, will never fully enjoy the fruits of their labor. They will never have the satisfaction that comes from deciding your own destiny.

Even while I was working for a living, whether it was at a butcher shop, selling newspapers and magazine subscriptions door to door, or as a Kelly Girl (later known as Kelly Services), I was deciding my own destiny, which means having control of my own money. It is up to you to decide what effect marriage or cohabitation will have on your money, and therefore your destiny.

I'm not trying to be confrontational or judgmental. None of this is, in fact, meant to help you make up your mind about whether you should get married or not. My intent is to make sure that you, the men out there, and you, the women out there, make as much money as you can, even before you've made some sober decisions about what your career will be.

And the reason, perhaps, the tone of what I say about marriage is sometimes brutal, always honest, and sometimes even funny, is that marriage has been, continues to be and will probably always be the best of all worlds and the worst of all worlds. The good, the bad and the ugly. If men and women were able to separate love from money, then perhaps more people would stay married. The only two things wrong with marriage for men are the following: 1) He can't have access to any other females (by law) and 2) If he does, he has to pay his wife more money for sharing his bed than he has to pay his mother for giving him life.

Oprah and Martha...neither is married. Oprah and Martha (before her legal troubles) were each worth hundreds of millions of dollars. At their rate of growth, they would soon be billionairesses... It's all theirs, the whole pie. If it's OK for them and they figured it out, you should too. But consider this: Do you think it's just coincidence that neither is married?

The great feminist Gloria Steinem eventually got married. She had been saying for years that it was time to stop depending on

# WORDS DO MEAN SOMETHING

I never imagined myself getting married. I have never been married. I suspect I will never get married. I believe in saying what I mean and meaning what I say, which means: words DO mean something. An oath you take should hold you accountable. An oath doesn't mean you can change your mind. The marriage oath IS sacred. I believe in it. I simply don't believe I can live up to it. I also don't believe MAN, by nature can live up to it.

I never wanted to take an oath I didn't think I could keep. I also thought I never wanted children. I find it curious, now that I have two wonderful children, that I would have ever felt that way. I don't have a biological clock. I don't have child-bearing hips. I don't "know" what women seem to know. Or I choose not to know.

The real reason I never wanted kids was I didn't want to turn into my father. He left my mother and me when I was almost seven. He passed away two years ago. I supported him the same way I keep supporting my mother. I bought both of them their own houses and paid all their monthly bills.

But was my father's absence any indication of what I would do if I had children? Was it biological? Did the wanderlust run through my veins? I never wanted to have children, because I never wanted to abandon them. I doubted myself.

The young man holding my hand as I'm about to get onstage in 1990 is one-and-a-half-year-old Nicholas Adam Tweed Simmons. He is the son I never thought I would have. I would later meet and fall hopelessly in love with my daughter Sophie Alexandra Tweed Simmons to an extent I never thought possible.

Nick is now fourteen and Sophie is ten-and-a-half.

I'm still here.

I WILL be here.

Today. Tomorrow. Forever.

men, women had arrived...and eventually she got married. Women tend to go for a guy who earns more money, is taller than she is and has more power. For her, that's a good match. You want a guy who's shorter than you, has less money than you, and is younger than you? I don't think so. By the way, men think the same thing. A good match for a man is a woman who is not as tall as he is, is less powerful than he is, and has less money than he does. That's also his idea of a good match.

I know some women support men. They've been had! He can go out and make his own money. So can you!

So ladies...what's it all about? Well, here it is...you can't pee like a puppy if you want to run with the wolves.

The choice for women is either to rely on sex and marriage as the way to get riches, or compete with men on their level (no "women's rules" like "women's basketball" or "midget rules.") Either you can go toe to toe with men or you can't play basketball. Same rules for men *and* women.

This is not as bleak as it sounds. We don't live in caves anymore and the strongest (men) don't necessarily win. As I said, the information age—computers—has leveled the playing field. Women can outperform and out-earn men.

Women, however, are almost non-existent in engineering, architecture, mathematics, the sciences, but especially the computer world. Why? You tell me. If computers are something you women have avoided, then the riches they offer (information, access and especially money) will avoid you. Women statistically tend to shy away from technology. I'm here to tell the ladies the computer will give you muscles just as big as the guys have.

And you can go online shopping as well! (Sorry, couldn't resist.)

So I say to you: does waiting for your husband to get home from work sound horrible to you? Then get off your ass and go do something. Stop relying on your looks. Go to school. Get a job. You can have it all. Just like the men.

\*　　\*　　\*

Tall buildings stand firm if the basement and the first floor are solid. It's never how tall a building is; it's only whether or not the foundation is solid. The problem with relationships is both men and women have dominion over each other. There's a judge and jury. Someone can ask you, "Where are you going? Where have you been?" My first response to the question "Where have you been?" is *"Who wants to know?"* People only want to know where you've been to find out if you've been with someone else. If man or woman is late by an hour or so, but especially the man, she wants to know where he's been. If she calls the office and he's not there she'll ask "Where have you been?" Who wants to know? What gives people the right to ask such questions? That's my problem with marriage. It eventually comes down to, Does somebody have dominion over you? And does somebody have their hand in your pocket? Whether they love you or not is beside the point.

No one has the right to ask me where I'm going. Nobody has that power. I'm a grownup; I'm fifty-three years old! The last person I had to answer to—my mother—had that right, because she gave me life! There is no one else who should be allowed to ask you that question; not men to women or women to men. The only exception is if I hire you and you are doing work for me I have the right to ask you where you've been, but only during the timeframe I pay your salary.

There are those men who are very jealous and possessive of their girlfriends, asking them where they've been and where they're going, keeping very close tabs on them. But these are men who don't have a lot of access to women. Guys who have a lot of girls don't really care. They're too busy dipping to notice what one individual girl is doing. It's when a guy has all his eggs in one basket that he holds on too tightly. Because there are no other females. If a guy's got a hundred girls he can call at any time he doesn't hold on as tightly.

It's like food. If you go to a buffet and there are other people eating, you don't care. But if you're starving and there's only one morsel of food, you will kill the other people to prevent them from getting that bit of food. Get it? Girls and food. When there's a lot of food on the table, other people can eat, no problem. When it affects you, we got a problem, Houston.

Money is like that too. If you've got a lot of money, you may not hold on as tight—which may or may not be a wise decision. But if you've only got a little bit of money and someone steals some of your pennies, it affects your life greatly.

\*　　\*　　\*

Guys like Dr. Phil are always telling you, "Find out what the relationship is all about." But he avoids the truth, which is that biology dictates behavior. "Oh, everyone else's husband is like that, not *my* husband." That's a lie. All men are created with the same basic DNA and have the same biological urges. And the divorce rate is high not because all these women are terrible, but because men wander. And I'm talking about the ones who have gone through divorces, who've paid the price for being caught "cheating." And how about all the multitudes of men who never get caught? Count all those up. Why do men keep doing it? Because we're designed that way—and if you have an argument, argue with God.

It reminds me of the story about a single woman who bought a little dog. She loved it with all her heart, fed it, walked it, fussed over it. One day she walked in and there was a pile of poop right in the middle of her nice carpet. She berated the dog, "How could you do this to me? I fed you, I walked you, I took care of you..." And the dog says, "Well, I never asked you to do any of that. And besides, if you didn't want poop on the carpet, why'd you get a dog? Lady, I'm a *dog*. You want peace and quiet, get a cat. I'm a dog, that's what I do—poop."

Yesterday I woke up and saw my dog, Snippet, who both Shannon and I love with all our hearts. Snippet was outside doing what he does naturally, which is trying to kill a squirrel. It was a Snippet I didn't recognize. My dog was clawing into the squirrel's back, and his nails seemed further out, and his teeth were bared. He was biting into the squirrel's neck. My immediate thought was, *How could you do this?* And I threw something at the dog to make him stop. Even after the dog was standing at attention and cowering, his teeth were still bared and he was snapping his jaw. The squirrel barely got away. And I was half-embarrassed by what I'd done, because if there was a word balloon like a comic strip over Snippet's head, the dog would have said something like, "What's your problem? I'm a dog. I was trying to kill the squirrel. That's what I do."

So why are men so attracted to women? Because we're MEN!

And women *know* all this! The truth is when women get together to play mah-jongg they say "All men are dogs." And that's correct. The lie is that "All men are that way except my husband. My guy isn't like that." When the lights go out and women are about to fall asleep they know it's a lie. They whisper to themselves, "Why are all men alike?" That's when the truth comes out.

And in the great cosmic plan I offer the following, and let someone else tell me what it all means. In the course of a lifetime of a woman, by and large, she has no problem having one monogamous relationship. If and when—and it's most likely when—a relationship has run its course, usually sooner than she would like it to end, she will get into another relationship. In her lifetime she will have a series of men lined up, one right after the other. Very few women nowadays have only one lifelong relationship. You will

have had multiple partners by the time your life is over. And it's OK, no matter how many oaths you take, you're fine with breaking them. Lying to God, the church and state and everybody else, because you're doing it from your heart. So you are completely ethical in your own view of yourself, which is to say you can line them up one right after the next.

Now men are just like women, except we line partners up at the same time. We have a line that goes left to right; you have a line that only goes forward. And I offer the following: What the fuck's the difference? All of us have multiple partners. Women's only objection is that men are willing to have another *partner at the same time you're here*. That's your only problem. You're not saying you have a problem with multiple partners, you're only saying "Don't do it while I'm here." And if we do have more than one partner at the same time, women want money. That's what it's really all about. If you were an alien from another galaxy studying it, you'd say "What the hell's the difference?" You all have multiple partners—one has more, one has less. It's a space/time relationship. It's OK for men to have multiple partners—just not at the same time. Well, tell you what, you pay attention to being a woman and we'll pay attention to being a man. We're not arguing with you that you can't have one right after another. Why are you arguing with us that we can't have them at the same time? Only because it involves you. You want to be the queen; the only one. The answer is NO.

It's all biology. There are exceptions—asexual men, gay men, lesbians and so on. But nature determines that women go for a provider because even if you plan your life a certain way, at a certain point when you get pregnant—and the tendency is that women *will* try to get pregnant—you're going to be out of commission for nine months.

Why were we designed this way? Why do women go out of their minds once a month? We all still have a prehensile tail. It's

**Message:**

*YES!*

Hey Gene! Thought I'd give you an update on what us crickets are up to.

We have a sample of the pistol box we'd like to send you. Should we ship to McGhees office? Please advise.

Other items we are working and waiting for info from various venders:

Lava lamp
Amp Bag
Money Bag
Directors Chair
Note Pad
Note Book
Address Book
Various clothing accessories

*ALSO — I WANT BLACK TOILET PAPER*

Dave and I have a number of other id... ...will present them to you as information... ...

Let us know about the box.

Later.

---

Around the time I was putting together the Kiss My Ass tribute album, I noticed the phrase "kiss my ass" elicited chuckles from people. They started making up jokes with the phrase. And it occurred to me that part of the "cool" quotient of merchandising is its humor—the notion that one shouldn't take one's self too seriously.

I thought Kiss My Ass toilet paper sounded like a good idea. I contacted offshore toilet paper manufacturing companies and did the price breakdown (the "price of goods"). I had them do different versions. One included our faces on the actual toilet paper you wiped with. That wound up being far too expensive and had potential repercussions: would the ink on our faces come off on your butt? Would it irritate?

So I went with a box that featured our faces (they were all different so you had to collect all of them). I also designed a cheaper version without a packaging box (shown here).

By this point I got so busy with everything else that was going on around us that I simply had to temporarily abandon the project. It was too time-consuming. As soon as I have some spare time, I will revisit Kiss My Ass toilet paper.

You can be sure in the near future you will have the opportunity to choose to wipe your butt with a different kind of toilet paper. Maybe one with my face in it.

right there, you can touch it. You don't need it, but it's there. We don't need fingernails to tear into flesh, but we still have them. We don't need canine teeth because food is all processed now, everything's a Slurpy. But the canine teeth are still right there in the front of our mouths to rip into flesh.

*      *      *

Men and women are not honest with each other. As long as that happens, the man will pay through his ass. You've got to tell each other everything. Tell a man everything, tell a woman everything. Before. Find out before. Don't have a plumber come over and fix your plumbing and then hand you a bill. Never do that. The same wisdom you use to make sure you get an assessment of the cost should apply to your relationships. I urge all men to find out what the cost of marriage is before they enter into it. Don't be shocked at the cost *afterwards*. Make no mistake about it, there is a cost to all relationships—even if you take a girl out to a movie. It's transportation, food and the cost of the movie. Sometimes the cost is agreeable—a man will say, I'm happy to take her out and spend the money and so on. But if the cost of taking her out is she wants a Porsche, he may want to know beforehand. "I went out with you, where's my Porsche?" You must know the costs of things beforehand.

My daughter said that to me when she was three. "Daddy, can I have a Porsche?" I said, "You can have the whole dealership." Giving is not the same as taking. I may want to give you the world. But if you try to *take* it, I'll fight you with every penny I have.

Women want men to buy them drinks. And marriage means I want a husband who will get up every day and go to work so I can have a house to live in and sit around and watch *I Love Lucy* reruns. And the more money that husband makes the better. More money means you have more access to that money. As I've stated,

MORE is a good word. When somebody has more money, he is more appealing. Men don't care if women want to contribute financially or not. We only care if you want some of our money or not. Because a man is not going to look to a woman and say, *You know what? I want to get married. I want her to go out and work for a living.* It's not the way we think. Men are self-sufficient. We only look to women for sex or companionship, take your pick. Women look to men for companionship and social security. That's the prime difference between men and women.

I would have no problem having a relationship with a woman who worked in the sanitation department. But I suspect a successful woman would not be anxious to have a relationship with a garbage collector. His job is a reflection of how attractive he is. That's not true for men. It's purely physical, by and large. More money makes a man more attractive. Once again, MORE is good.

Men don't care about women's jobs. They care if she has a big set of jugs and a nice ass. Remember! You wanted the truth!! It's biological, it's their physicality—the attraction of women for men is visual. Perhaps the attraction of men to women is physical, but it's also ethereal—they might like a certain man because he has a great sense of humor and so forth. I don't know how to tell women this, but I could give a shit whether she can crack a joke or not. That's just what I want—to go out on a date with a beautiful woman and have her break into Lucille Ball impressions. What women want men to do is to tell funny stories. We've got to be Bozo the Clown while you just sit there and smoke your Marlboro Lights. "I want a man with a sense of humor." You hear that all the time. How many men say, "I want a woman with a sense of humor?" We don't want you to be funny! We just want you to be sexy.

Don't be tomboys, playing baseball with us. You can't run, you can't throw. Let the guys play guys' rules. Men have to change the rules so the girls can play. By the way, guys beat up on small guys too. It's not about sexuality, it's nothing personal against women. It's that you can't run and throw like the guys do. A guy can't get on a football team if he's smaller. He can't say, *You're picking on me because I'm a guy.* Same rules apply to women. "You are a weakling; get off the team." You're picking on me because I'm a woman! OK, you're right. In nature there's only one set of rules. Only the strong survive.

There's an Olympic men's division. Now there's a women's division. Next there will be a pygmy division. There should be one division. Let the best man or woman win. The best of the best, that's what it should be about. Not the best of the Europeans or the best of the women. You know why the Japanese are never in the world heavyweight championships for boxing? Because they get knocked out. Just because they're smaller, racially? Yes! Women are not on that level, and the reason there are no heavyweight women boxers is because they'll get knocked out! It's politically correct, which is another way of saying "*bullshit.*" And girls, you can't be on the New York Yankees because you can't hit? "Just because I'm a girl?" Precisely because you *are*, yes!!

\*     \*     \*

Once again, I can't wait for my hate mail. And once again, I stand by my words.

Dr. Phil is on his way to millions, but only if he doesn't get divorced. And now that he's famous, he'd better not be caught in the arms of any of the countless new offers I'm sure he's gotten from a sea of new women who are attracted to him because he's (yes) good-looking, but (mostly) famous.

You read it here first!

"George Washington slept here" may be far more historically profound than you might realize!

Two women are talking. One says,

"We women have to go through menstrual cramps and childbirth... What do men get?"

The other says, "Us."

# Again...

- Are you a male, any age, about to get married? DON'T! Not now, not ever!

- Are you a female, any age, looking to get married as soon as possible and as often as possible? GREAT! Keep doing it! Get married lots of times! (You can also have a job and keep that money as well.)

- Are you a female with joint bank accounts, credit accounts, joint everything with your first husband and every single husband you will ever have? GREAT! Good for you! (Bad for him.)

- What is the cost of taking a woman out? Of living with her? Of marrying her?

# CHAPTER SEVEN

# Taking Care of Business

**B**y the mid-80s Paul and I noticed that although we were making more money than we'd ever made before, there were still some unanswered questions. Paul brought in an outside source who, after making some inquiries, decided there might be trouble in paradise. After all the legal wranglings back and forth, our then-business managers were forced to leave, and after suing them, we were awarded cash and punitive damages.

Being self-managed meant different things to Paul and myself. We have different interests, different things we're willing to do, and different strengths. Paul has always been much more firmly rooted in the image and credibility of the music of KISS. I was never all that much concerned with credibility. I believed if we stood the test of time, that was enough. I was always much more interested in the business of KISS. Although the songs were certainly important to me, what it all meant to a group of critics never played a big part in my life. It's all delusional anyway, because to your mom it all sounds the same. Even the notion of credibility to people who never went to music school and can't read or write musical notation is lunacy, at best.

I was left with only myself to look to for all sorts of decisions. I found myself in the often awkward position of calling booking agents and doing things I'd never done before, including booking a South American tour and a Japanese tour. I also negotiated with recording studios, engineers and producers and tried to keep the cost of doing business to a minimum. I often argued ad nauseum with recording studios about the cost of tape and/or the cost of the daily recording session.

You must learn to make money for yourself and handle it properly. You should be loose, be fancy, be free, be liquid (have money), and be as flexible as possible. On Wall Street, the classic investment portfolio wisdom is (if you're fairly conservative) start by taking a look at the money that you have in hand. Not your earnings potential, but *cash in hand*. And if you want to invest, the worst place in the world is at a savings bank, because what they give you doesn't take inflation into account. You'll never make as much in a savings bank as you would being a little more adventurous with your money. A bank is completely safe. It's covered by the FDIC (Federal Deposit Insurance Corporation). They have to pay you your money, or the federal government will step in and make the bank solvent and make good on your money.

But inflation will outperform the money you're making in interest (which, by the way, you have to pay tax on). The choices you have are being very conservative, a little conservative, or adventurous. If you're not enormously rich, then don't be adventurous. Don't put all your money in steel or gold or diamonds or any *one thing*. Because it goes against the grain of "Don't put all your eggs in one basket." You hear it all the time: "DIVERSIFY. Ten percent of this, ten percent of that." Mutual funds are good because they're a lot of different areas put into one.

But by and large the advice is to stay away from the stock market. If you don't have a lot of money, Wall Street won't love you as much as Bill Gates. Wall Street loves dollars, not pennies. Save, save and save some more.

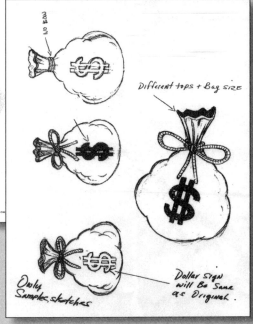

Different tops + Bag size

Dollar Sign
will Be Same
as Original.

Only
Samples sketches

I started to fool around with a few ideas about maximizing my moneybag logo. I wanted to do "moneybag" kisses, just like the Candy Kisses we all grew up with. I even tried to entice the Hershey chocolate people about doing a KISS Candy Kiss, but they wouldn't bite. So I pushed the moneybag kiss. It would look exactly like the aluminum paper-packaged Candy Kiss familiar to everyone. But they wouldn't bite on that idea, either.

So I started thinking that if I made the moneybag bigger, it might be cool to put it on a backpack. I still think this one's a winner. Who wouldn't want to wear that on their backs?

The only thing preventing the backpack from becoming a reality is what actually happens to ideas...all ideas. Either there is a delivery system and a store to sell your goods, or your fruit will rot on the trees. The point being, I may have the idea and design all done, but without a manufacturing/distribution company to produce it and a store to sell it, I have nothing—at least until I find a company to do it (and in the process, of course, pay me for the privilege of doing it).

All in due time.

# MAXIMIZE

One thing I've done right over the years is investing in the business I know best: Gene Simmons. Because while Enron and other corporations will be stealing, fiddling with the numbers and double dealing, I know Gene Simmons best. I know that I will work harder for me than anybody would. I'm willing to gamble on myself.

Having said that, I almost never use my own money in any entity I've ever been involved in. I always use somebody else's money. Always. Never use your own money—or hardly ever. Use your parents' money, the bank's money,

> One thing I've done **right** over the years is investing in the business I know **best: Gene Simmons.**

God's money, your girlfriend's money—use anybody's money, but don't use your own. Make a deal with them. The deal should be they give you the money (capital) and they need do nothing else. You will then go and work that money—that is, put in the time and effort. After costs (which also means that you get paid a pre-agreed-upon price for your labor) the profits, if any, will be split fifty-fifty with that person. And by the way, if you can get fifty percent of the profits for yourself, you're one lucky bastard. Because if you were using *my* money, I would want to keep ninety percent of the profits, and I would want to be paid first, even before expenses. I'd want to be paid on the first dollar in. *You* would pay the expenses.

However, and keep this in mind, people who have money are also fascinated by worker ants. Convince them you are the king of worker ants. They love to see other people scurrying about trying to build things. They want glory. They want to see their name up in lights, but they don't have the time and/or passion, perhaps, to put as much into it as you're willing to put into it. Which is why banks, foundations, economic institutions, and Wall Street are solely based on the notion that there are trillions of dollars somebody has to do something with. It's a stunning revelation.

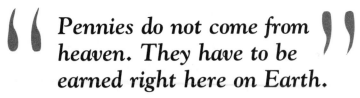

Nobody ever puts it that way, but the entire economic system is simply based on the notion that money must be spent! Otherwise, it dies. Money must keep being reinvested, otherwise inflation takes big bites out of it every year. The "money people" are dying to find somebody like you to give money to, if you're willing in exchange to put in your blood, sweat and tears. Don't forget time and effort, as well.

Good help is hard to find. If you're good help, money would love to find you. I want to pump you full of hope. I want to shake you inside out and make you realize that you, too can have access to the American Dream. I spell that dream C-A-S-H.

> *Pennies do not come from heaven. They have to be earned right here on Earth.*
> —MARGARET THATCHER

Note that she said pennies, not dollars.
It may take you awhile to understand this one:

> *If A equals success, then the formula is A equals X plus Y plus Z. X is work. Y is play. Z is keep your mouth shut.*
> —ALBERT EINSTEIN

In other words, as another famous person once said, I never learned anything while I was talking.

There are foolish ways of enjoying life, I'll grant you, and I'm not here to tell you that you shouldn't do them. I simply decided that being poor was not an acceptable alternative. I will scratch and claw my way to riches because the alternative is being poor.

George Raft, an American actor in the 1930s and '40s, went through $10 million. He said, "Part of the loot went for gambling, part for horses, and part for women. The rest I spent foolishly." *All* of Mr. Raft's spending habits were foolish. Ten million dollars is a lot of money, especially if you lose it.

Many people say money is the root of all evil. That's actually not true. *Lack* of money is the root of all evil. People will hold you up for money, but those same people, if they were loaded (rich), might not resort to holding a gun in front of your face.

Sometimes passion and perseverance are worth more than experience and qualification. Either way, if one is experienced and qualified, it helps to be passionate. And persevere! Never give up!

---

*I have always doodled. When I first set eyes on my first comic books, I not only admired the stories and the costumes, I became interested in the various styles of art. I was a big admirer of comic artists like: Al (Flash Gordon) Williamson, Frank (Conan) Frazetta, Steve (Spiderman) Ditko, Jack (Fantastic Four) Kirby and other lesser known artists like Reed Crandall, Gil Kane and loads of others. I came to know their styles within half a second of seeing a piece of art.*

*I started to approximate their styles. Sometimes I would be inspired by one of their creations and then draw my own version of it. I never traced.*

*I have hundreds of these pieces of art. When I showed a few of them to an art dealer, he proposed a "Gene Simmons Art Show" to be held at Caesar's Palace in Las Vegas. He proposed a series of limited lithographs (a few hundred each), signed and numbered.*

*He told me it would net in the millions.*

*I haven't gotten around to this new business, simply because so far I've only looked to my art as pleasure. But lest you think any less of me (or more, depending on your point of view), never fear. In the near future, I will take a good hard look at this possible new venture.*

*In the meantime, I thought you might like to see some of my doodles.*

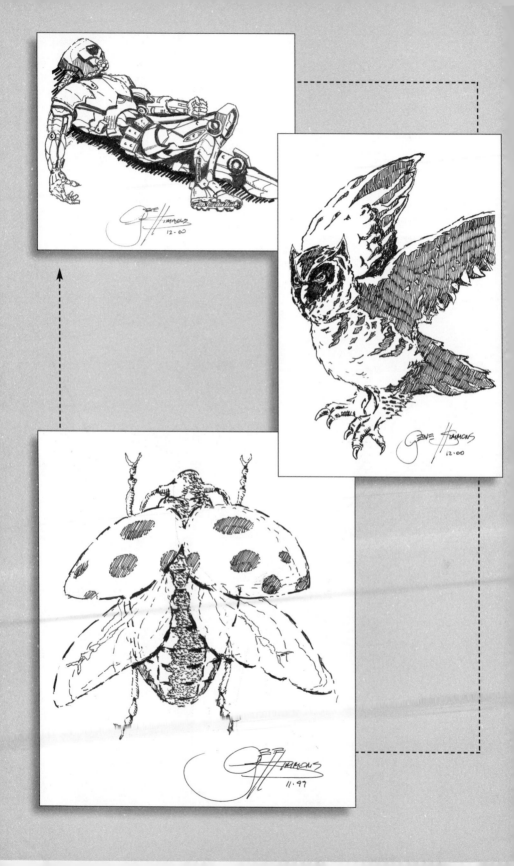

\*　　\*　　\*

I continued to produce other bands and act. I was offered another bad guy role in a movie called *Wanted: Dead or Alive* starring Rutger Hauer. In quick succession after that I acted in *Red Surf* with George Clooney (before his fame), *Never Too Young to Die*, *Trick or Treat* and, with Paul, the documentary *The Rise and Fall of Western Civilization*.

*In 1986 I was offered my second film—* Wanted: Dead or Alive, *opposite Rutger Hauer. The film company was New World. I met director Gary Sherman, who initially told me they were thinking of Charles Bronson as the good guy. I offered I didn't think it was a good idea. They eventually got Hauer.*

*On the first day of shooting on the set, Sherman got all the crew together and introduced me to Hauer in front of the entire cast and crew. Rutger was friendly, came over, grabbed each side of my face and cupped it in his hands. He proceeded to kiss me square on my mouth. I'm not sure why he did that, but it certainly elicited howls from everyone around us.*

*This time, my photo was allowed on the video cover right next to Rutger's. My film activities were causing divisions in the band in general and between Paul and me specifically. By 1986, we were playing with Eric Carr on drums and Bruce Kulick on lead guitar. We were doing well on tour and selling records.*

*We were always told by the peanut gallery to our left that without our patented KISS make-up and without Ace and Peter, the band couldn't exist. They were wrong then. They are wrong now. A team is always more important than any one member. No matter who it is. Yes. That includes me.*

I also tried television—the two hour premiere movie of the week of *Miami Vice*, HBO's *The Hitcher* and later on, *Talk to Me*, *Millennium* and a few others.

I wanted to stretch. I wanted to have my cake and eat it too. Also, although KISS had gone way beyond anyone's expectations, I didn't want to have all my eggs in one basket. My partner Paul, who was always concerned about KISS' music, expressed his concern that my outside activities were impacting on KISS.

KISS was still my passion. I immersed myself in areas that were left untouched. I was also a neophyte and wasn't exactly qualified to make legal judgments. Either way I wound up giving one of our auditors an entire breakdown of albums we never got paid on. Or, on albums that were sold at a discount price without our permission. I hunted down bootleggers and, with the help of lawyers, made a case against them.

I started collecting KISS fanzines, which by then numbered in the hundreds. Before the Internet, they were my eyes and ears around the world. They reported on all things KISS. Bootleg videos, bootleg records, bootleg merchandise and so on.

I stopped all illegal KISS comic books and managed to get all the original art. I noticed that dead celebrities had auctions and wondered why KISS couldn't have one while we were alive. Eventually I arranged and negotiated a deal for our own KISS auction that was held at Paramount Studios in Hollywood.

Over the years I noticed many KISS magazines appearing on the newsstands. I'm not a lawyer, and yet certain questions would pop up in my mind. For instance, the band owned its own make-up and logo, and the Trademark Office prevented anyone else from being able to (for instance) put out a KISS T-shirt without our permission and without our profit participation. Why, then, were publishers allowed to distribute their own KISS magazines without us being involved in at least an advisory capacity and without a profit participation? I was told that since we were public figures, any interference on our part would be tantamount to limiting the publisher's rights to "freedom of the press." I didn't agree.

I pushed my point with our lawyers and was advised that, yes, perhaps I had a case. Under the law, we certainly had a right to "first merchandising" status—before anyone could make a dime off of the band's trademarks, we should be the only ones (as owners of the trademark) to "earn a living" from it.

That opened the door for me to pick up the phone and call one of the more active KISS magazine publishers. They were understandably surprised to hear me on the other end. I told them that while it was all very nice to walk to the newsstands and see entire magazines devoted to KISS, it wasn't okay that we were not consulted about the content and, more importantly, the publishers were getting paid and we were not. I said that the reason I was calling, instead of lawyers, was simply as a pragmatic way of letting the publishers do what they wanted to do (publish the KISS magazines) and also to satisfy certain considerations we had. I was calling as a "deal-maker," not a "deal-breaker." In fact, I continued, if they gave us a healthy slice of the profits and an advance—nonrecoupable (we would keep the money whether the magazine was successful or not), their magazines would be "official" or "authorized"—in essence, a licensed KISS piece of merchandise, and I would keep the "barking dogs" (lawyers) away.

As far as I know, this has never happened before in the magazine world, but the publisher agreed. As a result, the publisher and the band put out ten different KISS Specials. All sold very well. The publisher was happy. And we got big, fat checks we wouldn't normally have gotten. Additionally, I made sure the publisher gave us free advertising pages to advertise whatever KISS merchandise we were selling at the time.

\* \* \*

It's fascinating what you can learn if you just keep your eyes and ears open. Originality is highly overrated. I don't have an original bone in my body. All I do is take stuff that everybody knows and put it together. When a chef says, "This is my original creation," he's lying. There's nothing new under the sun. He has just made up a new combination of ingredients. That's what I do. The truth is, what often works is simply what works, and whether it's original or not has very little to do with it. Many original ideas simply aren't pragmatic. Pragmatic means "leads to money." Lest I remind you too often, money is what this book is all about, it's what I'm all about, that's what *life* is all about, and that's what you should be all about!

> **Originality is highly overrated. I don't have an original bone in my body. All I do is take stuff that everybody knows and put it together.**

You can be original and poor. I'd rather be unoriginal and rich. How about you? Take originality as opposed to being pragmatic. Originality is just somebody looking for a pat on the back. I don't want a pat; I want your cash in my pocket. Pragmatism is potentially a harvest of cash. I don't want to be on the Lewis and Clark expedition and trailblaze. I want to be the guy who comes afterwards, after they've all been bitten by mosquitoes, and comfortably follow the trail they've made. I just want to do it better and cheaper and reap the rewards. I'm aware of and recognize the value of original thinkers and trailblazers. But unless I trademark and corner a market, do I want to be the Wright Brothers—then—or American Airlines—now?

NR 3-87 PRIS 21:50 I NORGE 27:- I FINLAND 21:-

# F&V

SCANDINAVIAN

FILM & VIDEO

- VI LOTTAR UT
- FILMBÖCKER
- SOUNDTRACKS

**Exklusivt!**
SHO KOSUGI GÅR
EN MATCH MOT F&V

**Biopremiärer**

- **PLUTONEN**
  SKAKANDE KRIGSDRAMA

- **"HEMMA-VÄRST"-**
  GÄNGET PÅ BIO

- **TRICK OR TREAT**
  FÖRSTA HÅRDROCK-RYSAREN

CENSUR **NIGHT OF
THE CREEPS**
- månadens skräckfilm

80-TALETS BAD GUYS

# GENE SIMMONS

ÄR I GOTT SÄLLSKAP MED RUTGER HAUER, MICHAEL IRONSIDE, SEAN PENN m fl

124-3

*After I had done a few movies—Runaway, Wanted: Dead or Alive, Trick Or Treat, Never Too Young to Die and Red Surf, I started to get press around the world focusing on Gene Simmons the actor and not Gene Simmons the rock star. Here is the cover of a magazine that appeared in Finland and Norway. The photo was taken after I had finished shooting a movie. My hair was growing back. I hoped it would grow back in time for the band's forthcoming tour.*

Pragmatism means if you're going to copy-cat something, do it where "who" or "what" you're copying is. Open your restaurant right next door to other successful restaurants. Just make yours different. It works. I like Chinese food, but not every day.

# Again...

- **You know yourself best and can count on yourself more than anyone. Are you investing in yourself, first and foremost?**

- **Are you good help? Would your work ethic impress people who might give you money?**

- **Have you stretched and grown throughout your working life? Are you constantly testing yourself, trying new things, setting new goals, learning about other areas of your business?**

*Santa makes a list and checks it twice, and so do most people who go grocery shopping. Years ago I started making a list of projects I was working on outside the normal "I'm in a band. All I do is record albums and tour." Every day we weren't on tour (physically away from my office/guest house) I would wake up in the morning and stare at the list. What haven't I done right? How can I improve on the deals? How and where am I going to find new ones?*

*During the years we didn't have a "manager" per se, I often found myself picking up the phone and going after the deals myself. I had an idea for a KISS tribute album after I saw a few bootleg KISS tribute albums released by fans. One in particular called Hard To Believe had, among bands paying tribute to us, Nirvana and The Melvins. I figured if there was ever going to be a KISS tribute album, why not put one together myself? I never use secretaries to make my calls or keep notes. I made a list that included a few hundred artists from rock and pop, old and new. I called all of them. More than once.*

92 REVENGE

✓ ALIVE III          [PROJECTS]
93
93 ✓ KISS MY ASS · LP + VIDEO

✓ KISSTORY · THE BOOK · BOO DIRECT · MUSIC MKTG

✓ KISSNATION · KISS vs. X·MEN

✓ KISS CONVENTIONS · DESIGN + EXECUTE

✓ SONY MERCH DEAL ·

CARTOON SHOW ·

ANIMATED MOVIE

✓ FEATURE FILM

KISS ON B'WAY

94 ✓ MTV UNPLUGGED · TV · ALBUM · VIDEO

94-5 ✓ S. AMER · JAP · AUST · TOUR + CONS

✓ ACE + PETER

95 ✓ DOC MCGEE DEAL

✓ FONE CARDS

✓ INT'L KISSMAGS WORLDWIDE

✓ PSYCHO CIRCUS COMIC · McFARLANE

✓ DOLLS · McFARLANE

✓ MUZAK

✓ DRUG FREE AMER

✓ SPIN

ROCK OF NATIONS

CD ROM

✓ AUDIT

AUCTION · WAREHOUSE CONSIGNMENT

* SKETCHERS. MK GREENBERG
BOZELL ADV. TOM BERNADIN
DPB - BOB KUPERMAN
SEGA - BARBERA JOYIENS
* CAPCOM - BILL GARDNER
GREY ADV. BOB SKOLLAR
ADIDAS - ROSS MCMULLIN
MIDWAY. NEIL NICASTRO
XM DAVE LOGAN
HEINZ MK MULLEN
HARMAN - JOE PULIN
* ELEC ARTS STEVE PERKISS
SONY COMP AMY BLAIR
BANDAI BILL BEEBE
BRISK/PEPSI RALPH SANTANA
c

* ACTIVISION DAN HAMMOND
GREY ADV. BOB SKOLLAR
OGILVY + MATHER MITCH KANNER
LIFESTYLES. CAROL CARROZA
SAATCHI + SAATCHI TODD SEISSER
BBDO PHIL DUSENBERRY
YOUNG + RUBICAM JIM FERGUSEN
* ARNOLD INTER PETER FANAT
* AVALON DALE THOMPSON
* MAINFRAME/-LOU NOVAK
* JIVE/SIMMONS RECORDS BARRY WEISS
* DARK HORSE MK RICHARDSON
* DC COMICS PAUL LEVITZ
RIOT ELEC - BRAD MARK
* STERLING MCF ALLEN TULLER
* UNIVERSE - RIZOLLI TERRY MANKALS
STREET JETS BARRY FLEISCHMAN
* LIGHTSPEED - GARY HASSAN
GAP. KEN PILOT.
JOSH - BARBERA JOYINS

*I had a title: Kiss My Ass. No one in our camp liked it. But, I persisted. I had interest from Ozzy with Stone Temple Pilots, Nine Inch Nails, Sir Mix-a-Lot, White Zombie and many more. When it finally got down to the list of artists who would participate, I started getting calls from managers and record company execs asking me if I was crazy to think they would let their artists be on a KISS tribute album without being paid enormous amounts of money. They found out I was offering little to nothing for actual recording costs, and the artists would receive pennies on the dollar of every royalty that came in. If an artist wanted to be on the record, I surmised, they wouldn't necessarily be doing it for monetary gain. At least I hoped.*

*The eventual list included Garth Brooks (who came onto the project because of Paul), Lenny Kravitz with Stevie Wonder and others. I walked into the record company president's office with Paul and said that I wanted KISS to be paid on the tribute album as if it were a KISS album (full advance of monies). A second album, KISS Alive III, would be recorded on the tour, and I wanted a full advance figure on that album as well. Remarkably, he agreed.*

*I also got the record company to let us put in a KISS merchandise advertisement in the album packaging for next to nothing. That way fans could pick up the album and, if they chose, buy other KISS stuff as well.*

*Kisstory was our nine-and-a-half pound coffee table book I put together in my guest house. To this day, I personally go down to the post office box, pick up the checks, sort through them and forward them on to our East Coast office. Kisstory was a huge success and keeps selling. Kisstory II followed and was a smash as well.*

*KISSNATION was the rebirth of the KISS/Marvel Comics relationship that spawned Marvel's biggest comics seller in the '70s. It was a comic-magazine. The comic book featured the KISS Meets the X-Men story by Gene Simmons and Mort Todd. I tracked down Stan Lee (the creator of most Marvel comics superheroes) and got him to write the dialogue. The magazine portion was put together in my guest house.*

*I persuaded Marvel to let me reprint the KISS Meets the X-Men comic book (without royalty overrides—meaning, they got nothing) in a KISS special magazine I negotiated with Sterling MacFadden. We received high five-figure advances for that magazine.*

*The KISS Conventions came about after I saw that the fans were doing their own and seemed to want the real thing. I got our legal team to trademark the phrase KISS Convention and KISSCON, so no one else could use it, and off we went on a one-of-a kind event that has yet to be duplicated by any band. We will be doing more KISS Conventions in the future.*

*The Licensing and Merchandising Deal came about when the head of the company came to visit us in the recording studio. I got him to agree that the new licensing and merchandising deal would encompass the next "without make-up" KISS tour, but he would not participate in certain "high-end" products such as our Kisstory book and the KISS leather jackets. He would also not have any claim on a "make-up" KISS tour, since we had absolutely no plans (as of that date) to do one. After all the deals were signed and he advanced us monies, he realized that the KISS Conventions weren't really addressed in the contracts. So he advanced us additional monies.*

*And when KISS went out on the KISS Reunion Tour, he had to pay us again.*

*I tried and continue to mount a KISS Cartoon Show.*

*I tried to get KISS on Broadway. It may still happen.*

WCW WRESTLER + LIC · MERCH FREE $_____
KISS CARTOON · FOX + LIC + MERCH $_____
KISSTORY II · $_____
AUCTION · $_____
DETROIT ROCK CITY NLC MOVIE · $_____
SOUNDTRACK · $_____
ROCK N ROLL ALL NITE · MOW · CBS $_____

ARENA FOOTBALL
NEW YRS SHOW - WCW - $_____
NEW YRS INTERNET - $_____

WCW DEMON WRESTLER
IMAGE DVD ·
VISA DEAL · w BILL
G.O.D. · DIGITAL · $
COSTUME DEAL $
GOT MILK -
NIKE TV AD · $_____
TOILET PAPER
2⅓' ACTION FIGURES - $
MAGAZINE · STARLOG - $
MAGAZINE · DETROIT FILMBOOK
MAGAZINE · PSYCHO CIRCUS 1 + 2 AND PAPERBACK
PLAYBOY COVER
I BEAM $_____

...DO IT YOURSELF

During the years we didn't really have a manager, I negotiated with booking agents for a South American tour, a Japanese tour and an Australian tour.

When Paul and I decided to get back with Ace and Peter, I was the one dispatched to sit down with them and make a deal. I flew to New York, asked our lawyer to exit the room, and I sat in there with their manager and made the deal. While it's true the deal kept changing because Ace and Peter kept going back on the agreed-upon areas, the deal was eventually nonetheless worked out.

We needed a manager for the Reunion Tour, and I negotiated our manager's profit participation.

A company came to us wanting to do KISS phone cards. I negotiated the deal.

I got Sterling MacFadden publishers to do a series of KISS magazines, with our cooperation, but only with the proviso that they advance us monies and only if we participated on a 50/50 basis. That relationship continues to be a win/win for all involved.

I tracked down Todd McFarlane and convinced him to put out a new series of KISS comics (KISS Psycho Circus comics), which lasted thirty-two issues. I also convinced him to put out KISS action figures. I negotiated the deal with him and got multiple seven-figure advances. The KISS line of action figures have been his greatest hit.

I accidentally met one of the executives of the elevator/dentist music company Muzak and made a deal on the spot. They would do middle-of-the-road versions of our songs for dentist's offices. And, why not...

WCW Wrestling and the Demon.

I read about Elvis and how his estate was holding an auction and I wondered why we couldn't do a KISS auction while we were still living. We had warehouses full of stuff we no longer used, and fans kept clamoring for a piece of it. Why not give them a chance to get some it, instead of letting some museum have it? I tracked down a few auction houses, got them bidding against each other for the rights and finally settled on a company that give us multiple seven-figure advances. The auction was held for the fans at Paramount Studios in Hollywood.

I produced Detroit Rock City, got the band the soundtrack and had the film company pay the band "underlying rights" fees as well as "performance fees."

A digital company came to me to discuss a KISS digital game. I met them at ICM talent agency and made a deal where they paid us high six-figure advances, non-recoupable. We also started getting paid from unit one sold. A deal, I'm told, cannot be made.

I found a buyer willing to pay us hundreds of thousands of dollars for a set of our outfits. KISS played Dodger Stadium in 1998. We stepped off the stage and gave the outfits to the buyer, who in return gave us the check.

I did a NIKE television ad that paid well.

There are countless other deals I have been involved with and continue to do. The fans hate that part of it. Some of the band members do, too. Tough. I found out long ago when there is no one else who is willing or capable of making these deals, there remains no one else I can turn to. I have to do it.

If you want something done right, the saying goes, you may as well do it yourself.

# CHAPTER EIGHT

# Born Again

By 1994 we had existed without Ace Frehley and Peter Criss, two of our original members, for fourteen years! We had also gone through a few other replacements as well. The band had undergone a metamorphosis of sorts. The make-up had come off. Possibly our biggest and most recognizable asset—the make-up and the out-fits—had been put aside. KISS without make-up was not as big a merchandising phenomenon as KISS with make-up. Nonetheless, we made the best of it. We had our logo and often, that was enough.

By the mid-nineties I noticed that the fan base had grown so enormous that the "worship of KISS," if you will, had started to become a reality. The fans started to tattoo their bodies with KISS images. KISS tribute bands started popping up all over the coun-try—all over the world, for that matter. Most intriguing were KISS conventions. I had never been to one, until we decided to call the local police outside of Detroit, Michigan and swoop down on a cer-tain KISS fan convention where they were selling stolen goods—pieces of costumes that had been stolen from us over the years. The SWAT team descended on the convention and took possession of the items.

While we were inside I got a firsthand look at how unique these gatherings were. It was a real eye-opener. The fans couldn't believe we were there, for one thing. After we left, the image of all those fans gathered together in a sort of "nationhood" was indelibly etched in my mind. When I got back home I started to do more research. I found out that KISS conventions existed not only in Detroit, Michigan but were held semi-annually in most major cities in America and around the world—in the Scandinavian countries, Japan and Australia.

Let's go back to the idea of supply and demand for a moment. If there was a demand, I sure as hell wanted to be the one who would supply it. Again, you don't need experience to do many things. You can learn as you go along. It was clear that the job of putting on our own official KISS conventions would be much bigger than I could handle all by myself. One of the first things I did was have our lawyers trademark the phrase "KISS CONVENTION" and "KISS CON" to ensure that only we were allowed to use the logo and phrase. This differentiated our conventions from the fan-run shows, which from that point on were forced to use other words such as "expo" or "show" to describe their own self-styled gatherings.

> Let's go back to the idea of **supply and demand** for a moment. If there was a demand, **I sure as hell** wanted to be the one who would supply it. Again, you don't need experience to do many things. You can learn as you go along.

After I received the official rights to the words, I contacted Tommy Thayer, the guitarist/songwriter from the group Black 'N Blue. They had a recording deal with Geffen Records but for the most part had run their course. They were just about to disband. I had produced the last two Black 'N Blue albums, and in the course of working with the band noticed that Tommy Thayer was well-

organized, diligent and a "can-do" kind of guy.

We had a heart-to-heart discussion and I told him bluntly that in case he hadn't noticed, his band was on its last legs and he had some serious decisions to make about his life and his future. What did he want to do? Did he have any plans? He wasn't sure. His options were open, he said. I said to him, "I'd like to offer you a job, but I'm not sure what it will entail. It may start off with me asking you to get me some coffee. The sky's the limit." He would be working for the band.

I told him to think about it; that this job I was offering would pay minimal cash initially and I'd be making it up as we went along. There would be no office hours as such, but I could call him twenty-four hours a day; and he likewise could call me twenty-four hours a day. I didn't want to hear about girlfriends, or walking the dog, or any other excuses. I, too, would work at all times. He would not take vacations or weekends off—same for me. You'll notice that this goes completely against the grain of what we're all taught—the five-day work week with weekends and a two-week vacation each year—which is, as far as I'm concerned, a recipe for disaster. You snooze you lose. I don't want to snooze, and I certainly don't want to lose. I don't want anyone around me who likes to snooze, because if they snooze, I lose. No snoozers allowed, and certainly no losers!

Tommy Thayer, to his credit, came back and said, "I'm ready. Whatever needs to be done I'll do." So I sat him down and took him through my thoughts. I said, "I want to do conventions. Here's what I want to do: take the twenty-five biggest markets in America, all the major cities. I'm going to send you on a plane trip to each of them, and you're going to contact hotels. Not necessarily the A-list, five-star hotels, but certainly convenient, mid-town hotels, easily accessible to the largest population. Get me prices on what it costs to rent out the ballroom for a twelve-hour period."

I had given this some thought. We didn't have a manager; therefore ten to twenty percent of our gross wouldn't go flying out the window to somebody else. We also weren't necessarily using a booking agency, which was another ten percent saved. We didn't have Ace and Peter to split with. It was just Paul and myself. There was everything to gain and nothing to lose. I decided the following: that we would hold our conventions in the ballrooms of hotels, that we would not get involved with hotel rooms, we would not sell food (I didn't want us to be responsible for any food-poisoning—one suit could wipe out the entire profit margin). I also didn't want to charge fans for parking, because just one car accident could result in a suit, and I didn't want to incur the expense of defending a suit, whether or not we won. The idea is to avoid an oncoming truck— it doesn't matter whose fault it is

I wanted to take over the ballroom of the hotel—a space big enough to hold as many as 2,000 people—for a twelve-hour period. For no reason whatsoever and only because I liked the number one hundred, I decided to charge $100 at the door. Now, everyone—fellow bandmates, friends, foes—told me that $100 was too much to charge. I stubbornly held my ground.

Thayer put together a small crew of guys who took some of our memorabilia and put together a Hall of Fame. Song lyrics, all kinds of things for fans to view. It was very similar to the Rock and Roll Hall of Fame, except this was the KISS Hall of Fame, and it traveled with us to our conventions.

KISS tribute bands were active all over the country, and though we owned the make-up, the logo and all the underlying rights, we simply let these tribute bands exist. We could easily have cease and desisted them with legal letters that would have forced them to stop their "illegal activities," but because they were fans first and foremost we let them carry on. It was now time for them to pay the piper. I instructed Tommy to call each one of these tribute bands. It would be their job to appear at the convention and put on a KISS-style show at no charge. The bands happily obliged, because though we didn't pay them to play, they were free the rest of the year to play clubs. A win/win situation for both sides.

When the very first convention was about to be mounted in Los Angeles, I got word that Peter Criss, who I hadn't seen since I'd asked him to appear on a Black 'N Blue album as a guest star a few years earlier, had called. He asked if he could bring his daughter to see some of the costumes and drums. His daughter had never actually seen KISS perform live, and he wanted her to at least see the displays. I got Peter's number and called him myself. I told him that KISS was here because of all four of us. Certainly we would be happy for him to bring his daughter to the convention and would in fact send a limousine to pick them up so he could arrive in style and make his daughter proud. I didn't think of it, but Eric Singer, our then-drummer, said, "Why don't you ask him to do a few songs with us? I'm sure the fans would really get off on it."

The idea of playing with Peter again hadn't even occurred to us. But I thought Eric was right, so I asked Peter. He was overjoyed and agreed. We rehearsed a few days together, and it was clear that Peter's drumming wasn't anywhere near what it had been. So we decided he should simply sing with us. Eric Singer would back him up on drums. When the first KISS Convention finally opened its doors, it was oversold. Packed with fans. When Peter walked onto the stage, the fans all flipped out. It was a very heartwarming moment for Paul and me. We looked at each other, incredulous that Peter looked so bright-eyed and bushy-tailed and, for all intents and purposes, healthy.

Our responsibility at the conventions—Paul's and mine, along with Eric Singer and Bruce Kulick—was to show up for a few hours, answer questions, play a little unplugged, take requests from the fans and sign autographs. We averaged anywhere from one to two thousand fans per show. Above and beyond everything, a good time was had by all. Everyone enjoyed the gathering. It was the first time I'm aware of that any band has ever mounted their own conventions.

> **When the first KISS Convention finally opened its doors, it was oversold. Packed with fans. When Peter walked onto the stage, the fans all flipped out.**

The conventions were so successful that they immediately caught the attention of the press and other rock bands. When asked, I quietly pointed out what worked for us might not work for someone else. The other bands wisely stayed away from it.

The conventions were a one-of-a-kind success. Tommy Thayer

went from rock musician to working on conventions, to coming on tour with KISS and being chief cook, bottle-washer, and whatever came up. Today he is our tour manager. He also has a small record imprint called Eon Records—a name I gave him—and has bought himself a house and more than one very nice car. Tommy's done well for himself because above and beyond his due diligence and talent, he has the "can-do" philosophy.

The work habits you get accustomed to when you're a kid are the habits you will most likely practice when you become an adult, when things really count. If you have the philosophy that no matter what, you should do a good job, the rewards will speak for themselves. You will get promotions, you will make more money, other people will want to hire you, and ultimately, if you're lucky, you'll get your own business. And when you're the boss and are actually paying the bills, you will want to hire people who have your philosophies. That means good workers who have the integrity to do a good job, even if they don't like the job.

> **If at the core of every thought you have, when you wake up in the morning and go to sleep at night, is *How can I make more money?* You will be shocked at how much more money you will make.**

So when you're a kid playing in a small band, there is no difference, philosophically speaking, between being a kid in that local bar band or being in KISS. You should put in the same amount of effort and you should take the same amount of pride in your work. When I was a kid publishing my fanzines I had the same work ethic and the same drive as I do now that I own my own magazine, *Gene Simmons Tongue*. The same philosophy I had as a little kid of having more than one girlfriend, and sometimes letting her pay or going Dutch, is the same philosophy I have today, which is that I refuse to pay for companionship.

Everything in your life should be a modus operandi, "way of doing things." A motivation that kicks in, a certain behavioral pattern. If at the core of every thought you have, when you wake up in the morning and go to sleep at night, is *How can I make more money?* You will be shocked at how much more money you will make. You will make more money by spending less, certainly, but your mind will also work in completely different ways.

\*     \*     \*

At the same time we were considering our options for the future, we continued on without a manager. And aside from noticing that there was something new called the Internet, I also noticed there were many KISS books that came out about the band. Usually most of them were cursory and fan-oriented. It became clear to me that the time was right for us to do our own book. If you want a party, don't wait for someone to throw it for you. Throw your own party.

I called one of our legal advisors in New York City and asked him to set up meetings for me with different book publishers. I met many of them. Everyone had a story. After I did the arithmetic, it seemed that we would wind up netting out something like five percent of adjusted gross and/or net, depending on how you define it. It didn't seem like much money, even at the high end of our escalation clauses (which means that percentages go up as the sales go up). Even if we achieved ten percent of net, the truth was, net was defined as "after the stores took their fifty percent off the top, after the publishing company paid for distribution, printing and other costs." "After" followed the word "after" followed by still another

Through the years I learned that even though I was the guy onstage that stuck his tongue out and threw up blood, what went on in record company board rooms was equally as important. And even though my relationship with my band mates and management was something I had to pay a lot of attention to, the people who manufactured and distributed the records also needed attention. It meant a phone call every once in awhile to thank them for their support. We all did that. Or calling a radio station manager to kibitz (kid around). The everyday people who made things work were important, but of utmost import were the people who were the bosses. Inevitably, they were the people would decide everything. How much they were willing to pay (in advances) and so on.

Here I am with Alain Levy, then chairman of Polygram Records, the worldwide entity that owned Mercury (our label), A&M Records, Motown and others. Levy and I were never close enough to call each other "friend." But on occasion, especially public occasions, I would make it a point to search him out and go over to say hello.

As the chairman of a record company Levy was expected to go over to the talent on his labels and make them feel at home. Most artists would wait for him to come over. For me to walk over to him was to give him deference—"respect" in public.

Little things like that can help you in life. They have me.

A little goes a long way.

"after." Then perhaps you'd end up at the word "net," which meant that you'd get very few pennies, while everybody else got dollars.

So, foolishly or not, I decided to embark on self-publishing a book to be called *Kisstory*. It would be financed by us. The only experience I'd ever had in self-publishing and self-distributing was with my fanzines when I was thirteen. Before I knew anything about what the book would look like, how and where it would be manufactured, how it would be sold, or what it was going to cost, I settled on the title *Kisstory*, because this was going to be a history of KISS.

I continued to make inquiries with bookstores and publishers. I sat with representatives from Penguin Putnam, among others, and tried to convince them that we had a huge fan base and the book's potential was huge. The doors to the ivory towers remained closed. But that's OK—remember, you snooze, you lose. I learned that most publishing houses were based on the loss-leader principle. They had to amortize—that is, the winners had to pay for the losers, and even while they were busy planning their own books, there was a staff that had to be paid, rent to be paid for office space, and on and on. It was very expensive to produce books and very hard to make money on them.

I decided to publish the book as a cottage industry. The guesthouse on my property in Beverly Hills would serve as the editorial offices and layout room, so, no rent! The entire staff would consist of only one other person besides myself. My first decision was that the price of *Kisstory* would be $158.95. That was all I knew at that point. Remember, there was no content, no writer, nothing yet.

I had come across a young lady by the name of Susan McEowen. She was married, lived someplace outside of Indianapolis, and had worked on Rand McNally maps. I found her because I had initially approached the Rand McNally company about publishing a book. I envisioned it as being big, over-the-top, and weighing more than ten pounds, like their oversized map books. They didn't understand my concept. They understood maps. But through them I found Susan McEowen.

I asked her to send us a sample of her work, and she sent us some very basic KISS designs. Paul and I looked at them and immediately thought she had something. I got her on the phone (remember, I don't use secretaries). At first she didn't believe it was me calling. I told her the who, what, when, where and how. She was to get on a plane and come to Los Angeles. I didn't care if she left her husband or brought him with her; I didn't want to know about her domestic arrangements. I didn't care about any of that. This was an opportunity for her to work on a book. We would find out together what it was going to be. She would work out of my guesthouse and figure out for herself what her life would be like in LA. I didn't want to know about anything else—just be here by Monday.

She left her husband and dogs and for all I know, her dirty laundry and got on a plane. She appeared in Los Angeles ready to work. After a few false starts with art school students who wanted a shot at working on the book, Susan came in and reworked one of the art school ads that was a pastiche of all kinds of photos and designs. We worked together to create an ad. We sent it out to fan magazines, as a flyer to fans, and started taking orders for our book, before the book had even started to take shape!

I rented out a Post Office Box for $30 a month. I was then, and continue to be, the person who goes down and picks up every check, counts it and sends it to our office. The fans believed then, as they do now, that for their $158.95 they would get bang for their buck. It was our responsibility to deliver. The book, I decided, would be over a foot and a quarter long, more than a foot wide, and more than 450 pages. It would be the finest quality printing and binding, contain thousands of photos, and come in a hard shell case with embossed printing.

The book was not sold in bookstores (who would *normally* take fifty percent of the sale price) or through a distributor. There was no publishing house, which normally took the lion's share of profits to split with. A few fan writers did interviews with Paul and myself and received a one-time fee of a few thousand dollars for their work, but for the most part the book was pure net profit. With more than 90,000 books sold to date *Kisstory* has made almost twelve million dollars. I went against the wisdom of the publishing world that said the marketplace wouldn't bear a $158.95 book. I didn't agree with my bandmates that it was too expensive and should cost somewhere around $50 or $75. I stubbornly stuck to the notion that it was never the price but only whether or not you got bang for your buck.

Remember, no matter how good or bad the times are, you can buy a Volkswagen or a Rolls-Royce. They both get you to where you want to go; it just depends whether or not you want the quality of a Rolls. One of the reasons I wanted to self-publish *Kisstory* was to make sure the soft-cover versions and discount versions wouldn't come out—that you wouldn't be able to walk into bookstores and find an abridged softcover version. That would dilute the book's value. I wanted *Kisstory* to be the Rolls-Royce of books.

A Rolls-Royce costs about $500,000 today. There is no negotiation. You never see a Rolls-Royce dealership with a sign saying

> **Remember,** no matter how good or bad the times are, you can buy a Volkswagen or a Rolls-Royce. They both get you to where you want to go; it just depends whether or not you want the **quality** of a Rolls.

*SALE! 25% OFF!* The price of a Rolls is never discounted. It costs one price, take it or leave it. It has its value. You will get the respect you demand. If you haggle about the price on certain things it dilutes the value. Maybe it isn't worth that much, you might say. But you have to draw a line in the sand for something of value, and I decided that *Kisstory* was going to be something valuable. Not only did the book publishing world scratch its head and try to figure out this publishing anomaly, but we went on to prove that lightning can strike twice when we published *Kisstory II* a few years later. It, too, did very well, thank you. It also cost $158.95 and looked like the companion to the *Kiss Encyclopedia*. Eventually it will be. *Kisstory* will consist of ten volumes in all. Wait and see.

> **Good attitudes,** a can-do philosophy and plain, old-fashioned **hard work** can reward you very handsomely— and that means **more money** in your pocket.

Susan McEowen, like Tommy Thayer before her, had seized the opportunity and won. Good attitudes, a can-do philosophy and plain, old-fashioned hard work can reward you very handsomely— and that means more money in your pocket.

You can earn these rewards too. When you're born in America you have access to free public schools and all the advantages. A Korean family (or take your pick of any immigrant population) moves here, penniless, and they can't speak English. They open up a fruit stand and work twenty-four hours a day. They're open seven days a week. They never close. We are willing to work only forty hours a week. Koreans are willing to work a million hours a week. They'll bring their children and their grandparents in to work. If not family members, they'll bring friends—there are different kinds of family relationships. The point is that what they teach you at business school—loss leaders, point of diminishing returns—is a figment of everyone's corporate imagination. Think outside the box.

Be available (to work) twenty-four hours a day. You should be flexible enough to jump out of bed at 3 A.M. if your phone rings and opportunity knocks.

> **Be available (to work) twenty-four hours a day. You should be flexible enough to jump out of bed at 3A.M. if your phone rings and opportunity knocks.**

My children, in my will, will not get a windfall of money at one time. At a certain age they'll get a little bit. Just enough to get them by. I won't let them blow it. Every ten years there will be enough to last for another ten years. They're going to get up every morning and go to work. Because, at the heart of it, working is its own reward.

\* \* \*

What resulted directly from the conventions was not only the KISS MTV Unplugged album that went gold and made us more millions of dollars; it also caused us to find Ace and Peter again.

The KISS Conventions continued throughout America. By the time we got to Michigan, MTV had gotten wind of these events. They wanted to send a film crew to the Detroit Convention because we were playing at the conventions, and they thought it would make a great Unplugged segment. We decided to have them come to the New York show when the KISS

SILVER OR SHINY METALLIC

KISS SNEAKER

*These are drawings I made for a possible KISS Sneaker design. I started pitching every major sneaker company about the idea. I'd pick up the phone, track down the president of a company and start talking. My calls were usually met with comments like "Alright. Who is this, really?" Again, I never liked using secretaries to make calls for me. Not then. Not now. I just won't. I find it too impersonal. If I have something to say to someone, I'm happy to pick up the phone and dial them myself. At the very least, the person on the other end knows I'm committing my time and effort.*

*Regardless of the initial interest from the top sneaker companies, I couldn't close on a deal for us. So I started doing research into where sneakers were made. I found that almost without exception sneakers were manufactured in Korea. I tracked down a few manufacturing companies and started getting quotes based on my design. The prices came back very competitive.*

*After I figured out how much it would cost per unit and how much the price per unit went down as the number of units manufactured went up, I offered the numbers to the band. We wound up not doing it. There was a gamble in a product like this, having to do with too many variables. It wasn't like manufacturing and distributing Kisstory, for instance. Our book was "one size fits all." Sneakers, on the other hand, could come in any number of designs and sizes. And I knew nothing about the distribution system for shoes and sneakers. In brief, there were just too many variables.*

*But simply talking about it in this book might be just the impetus needed to push a sneaker exec into making a deal with us.*

*I haven't given up on a KISS Sneaker. Not yet. Not ever.*

Convention stopped there, in order to give us another few weeks to think about which songs we would play. When we got close enough to New York it was obvious we would have to call Ace and at least invite him to get up on stage the same way Peter had. Unbeknownst to us, Ace had spoken with Peter, who told him that the experience of getting up on stage with us again was a joy, and that he would highly recommend it.

When the original KISS lineup played on MTV's *Unplugged*— although without make-up—the reaction was immediate and overwhelming. The KISS *MTV Unplugged* album resulted; it went on to be certified gold. Even though the Bruce Kulick/Eric Singer/Paul Stanley/Gene Simmons lineup of KISS was ongoing at the time (we were finishing a new album called *Carnival of Souls*), it was clear that we should consider getting together for a reunion tour.

I called up Ace and Peter's then-manager, George Sewitt, who had at one point worked security for KISS. I flew to New York and asked Sewitt to meet me at our lawyer's office. I asked our lawyer to leave the room and I sat alone with Sewitt. I got to the bottom line quickly. I spoke with Sewitt face to face: just the two of us, to cut through all the legalese. Legalese is a peculiar language that exists in America. It's who uses it that makes it recognizable or not. The basic agenda of lawyers, well-meaning or otherwise, is the more of your time they use up and the more words they use to say something, the more they can bill you. A lawyer does not necessarily have a fiduciary duty—that is to say, an obligation to keep your costs down. By and large the nature of their job is to keep the clock running. Even though we had terrific legal representation, I wanted to show Sewitt that no matter what the lawyers said, they would still have to come back to us, and we wanted to cut through it all and draw a line in the sand.

He came back and said it was a deal. Ace and Peter flew out to Los Angeles. Everyone was cordial to each other, but in short order

Ace took the lead in going back on his word (as he had since the first day he joined the band) and changing the numbers. Peter quickly followed, and it ping-ponged back and forth, with the numbers going up and up. It was impossible to make a straight deal with either them or their representatives.

The very first show of our 1995 KISS Reunion tour that our manager Doc McGhee put on sale was Tiger Stadium in Detroit, which sold out in forty-seven minutes. We were unstoppable—55,000 tickets sold in under an hour. Not only did KISS come back and become the number one grossing tour in the world, but domino-effect-like, the licensing and merchandising of action figures, comic books, ad infinitum really kicked in as never before. There were more greatest hits albums that became gold records; there were Pepsi commercials and Holiday Inn commercials; KISS was everywhere—at the Super Bowl and finally the Olympics with an audience of 3 billion people. But it all started with a little thing called KISS Conventions.

> **Maybe the lesson learned for me, and hopefully for you, is Keep your eyes and ears open.**

We all like to think that we know more than we actually do, when the truth is we actually don't. As much as I'd like to take the credit for this as some kind of great, grand design, I cannot. Maybe the lesson learned for me, and hopefully for you, is *Keep your eyes and ears open.*

KISS, this time with Ace and Peter, became the number one tour from '96-'98. Our good friend Garth Brooks was number two. By some estimates the tour took in over $100 million gross. To give you an idea of what other estimates have been, we played Tokyo Stadium on one of the reunion tours to almost 50,000 fans. Not counting tick-

Here I am in 1995 at a bowling alley I had rented to celebrate my own birthday. If you want a party, might as well throw one yourself. The entire bowling alley was taken over. On the first three lanes, I had a flat stage set up for Green Jello to perform in full stage gear. The lights were dimmed enough so that everyone looked good. James (Titanic) Cameron, Roseanne and Tom Arnold, Hugh Hefner, and lots of girls came. My favorite songs were being played over the sound system (from Ray Charles' "Georgia" to Easybeats' "Friday On My Mind"), and guests were invited not to buy me any birthday presents. I asked them to contribute to Pediatric AIDS instead. This photo was taken right after Paul, Ace, Peter and myself agreed to do the Reunion Tour, but before we started rehearsing or applying KISS make-up—notice the goatee. Someone handed me a newspaper with the headline "How to turn your friends into slaves." I'm not sure what they meant by that, but perhaps some of you might have an idea.

et sales, it was reported that KISS earned $1,200,000 from the sale of T-shirts alone at that one show.

*     *     *

We started talking about a studio album with our manager Doc McGhee. A circus theme started to rise to the surface. Once we settled on *Psycho Circus* as the title, I hunted down Todd McFarlane, creator of Spawn and publisher of his own line of comics (Image) and action figures (McFarlane Toys).

I stayed over in his hometown of Phoenix while the rest of the band went to the next city. I convinced him to do a brand new comics line to be called *KISS Psycho Circus*. I also convinced him to do the action figures. I negotiated the deal and in short order we not only owned the rights and characters to our comic book, but the original comic book art as well. And even though our merchandising company tried to negotiate a good royalty with McFarlane, I thought I could

> **The album promoted the tour, which promoted the comic book, which promoted the action figures. And that's spelled: A S-M-A-S-H.**

do better. I did. Substantially. To date, the *KISS Psycho Circus* line has been McFarlane's most successful and profitable line.

The importance of doing the comic book and action figures before the album and tour came out was synergy—the idea that one effects the other...like a domino effect. The album promoted the tour, which promoted the comic book, which promoted the action figures. And that's spelled: A S-M-A-S-H.

Once the tour was about to get underway, Doc McGhee urged

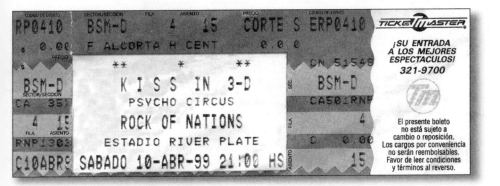

us to do a 3-D tour! It would be the first live, three-dimensional event of its time. You would get your tickets and a pair of 3-D glasses. Parts of the show projected on video screens in back of us were designed to pop right off the stage and visually assault you, even if you stood at the very back of the concert hall or stadium. The kick-off was at LA's Dodger Stadium on Halloween eve. It was also broadcast on Fox-TV as a special.

In the meantime, I arranged and negotiated for a buyer to pay us $250,000 for the costumes off our backs. We wore them once, handed them over and picked up our check.

Both Ace and Peter had suits they had to deal with, which we bailed them out of. Peter had recorded an album for a small label and the label made a financial claim against Peter. We helped him out. Ace had a big problem. We helped him out.

By the end of the first leg of the tour Peter fired his personal manager and then, eventually, so did Ace. Of course, the manager came after them for fees he thought were owed to him. Eventually it was settled.

Ace then decided to have his new girlfriend (who came on tour with us) become his liaison with the band. She would also be his "business manager" (Ace told me) and as such would have access to his financial records. The lady in question made such demands

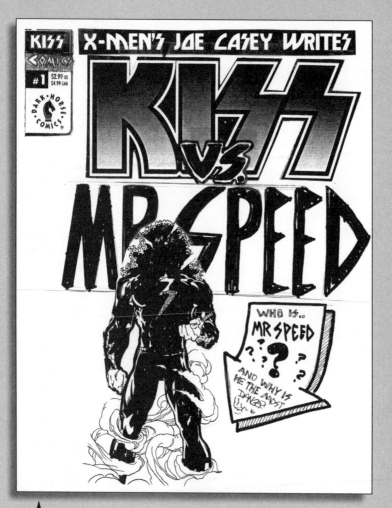

In 2001, after we finished running our course with KISS Pyscho Circus Comics, I went hunting for another comics publisher to put out a new generation of KISS Comics. I tracked down Mike Richardson, head of Dark Horse Comics, at the San Diego Comic Convention and over a weekend he and I came to a meeting of the minds.

Not only that, but at that same convention, I convinced DC Comics to team up KISS vs. Superman. They loved the idea at that time. They have since cooled to it. But anything's possible.

I had actually started thinking about doing my own line of comics—Simmons Comics. I convinced Mike to give it a go. I also convinced him to give each of our personas his own book—there would be The Demon comics and Starchild comics, etc. Four separate titles in all. Each book would come out a week apart, so that at the end of the year, each book would have twelve issues apiece.

The name of the venture then changed from Simmons Comics to KISS Comics/Dark Horse for political reasons. And after that change, Mike and I had a discussion about slowly introducing new characters. Let's start with a KISS Comic and then, in its pages, introduce new superheroes that could bounce into their own books.

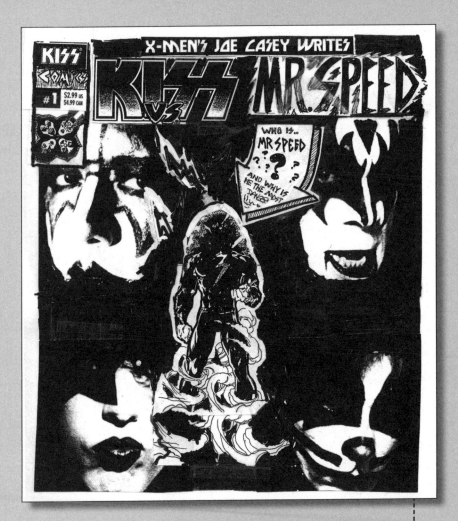

What you see here is my attempts at designing two different covers for the premiere of our new superhero, Mr. Speed. Yes, I know it's a title of one of Paul's songs. I always loved the sound of it, and it always struck me as a superhero name. I talked over the concept with our writer and presto! Mr. Speed is born.

The way I put together the layout was to use a black photocopy of the cover of our The Best of KISS CD. I then cut up the faces and moved them around so that they all seemed to be looking toward the center. I then photocopied one of Dark Horse's characters, blackened out the middle, put a lightning bolt in the center (since I didn't have a clue what the costume would look like at this early stage) and did two different versions. 1) I used the KISS faces around the figure. 2) I decided a "cleaner" look (without the big faces and black background) might "pop" more. I used the same small figure and simply blew it up. I used our KISS logo (taken from one of our tour books) and hand drew "vs. Mr. Speed" underneath.

As you read this, Mr. Speed has already made his appearance. And upcoming in the near future is Christine 16! She's an android—the 16th one. But, what were the other fifteen Christines like? Good? Bad? Stay tuned.

on everyone that she almost single-handedly succeeded in getting KISS banned from certain airports, airlines, and entire hotel chains that thought she represented the band. She also went through the concert hall and took notes on her notepad. She would then go to the road crew and give them instructions on how to change the show.

Ace eventually parted ways with her. She then started stalking Ace (he told me). The FBI were called in. Ace told me he called the young lady's father to try to stop the madness and, of course, we were in the middle of it all.

Ace then got another girlfriend, who also came on tour with us. She was nicer and basically stayed out of the way. However in short order she, too, left him.

Ace then decided he needed a bodyguard. A family friend of his came on tour with us. He would be our contact with Ace, we were told. We were to have no direct interactions with Ace. His bodyguard would pack up for him, get his coffee, and be the only person to speak to him. Somehow this guy wound up in front of the stage as part of our security team. We constantly tried to point out to him that he couldn't do that. For one thing, he wasn't insured and if he hit a fan, we would be liable. In any case we didn't want to hire him or have him represent the band. He would be Ace's companion, if he wanted to be, but he was to stay out of the band's business. It never worked. The agony continued. Ace and the bodyguard were charged $10,000 by a big Texas hotel for having indoor paint gun fights. Ace was taken to a hospital for a bullet fragment that was lodged in his chest when he went Uzi (Israeli machine gun) target practicing with his cousins. And eventually, of course, Ace forgot to pay his bodyguard his salary. The bodyguard asked me to intervene and ask Ace to pay him.

Every time we wanted to enter Canada to play a concert, the border patrol would check everyone's records and of course Ace's past would catch up with him—drugs and police problems. They didn't want to let him enter the country. It took a lot of effort to convince the authorities he had changed.

The stories are far too many and far too long to go into here. In fact, they are endless. It's also difficult to believe even one, not to mention all of them. But they all happened. Including Peter being arrested in a New York airport for carrying a gun in his luggage. Why he did that and what his story was, I can't say.

When it was time to enter the studio to record *Psycho Circus*, we decided we needed an outside producer to decide everything: which songs would be recorded, where they would be recorded and so on. But before we even began rehearsing and reviewing the material, Ace and Peter decided it was time to renegotiate their contracts yet again. They refused to start recording until they got what they wanted.

> The **reason** I mention some of these stories is to illustrate that your pattern of behavior either has a **positive** effect on your cash or a **negative** one.

The reason I mention some of these stories is to illustrate that your pattern of behavior either has a positive effect on your cash or a negative one.

\*     \*     \*

New Year's Eve 1999-2000 KISS played at Vancouver Stadium. We hugged and wished each other well for the new century. Two days later, we went to Alaska to do a show. It was the first time we had visited Alaska since our first tour in 1974, when we had played there third on the bill to Savoy Brown and Manfred Mann. For all intents and purposes, we returned as the conquering heroes.

We had become icons: comic books, licensing, and merchandising. We had broken attendance records set by Elvis and the Beatles and had more Gold Album Awards than any other American band in history.

We decided to go out on top. At least that's what we told each other. Paul and I had a five-year plan, as stated in the contracts. We would have taken it further, but it was becoming very plain that the steam was running out of the band.

The Farewell Tour was agonizing. The relationships were strained. There were new demands put on the band by Ace and Peter. By this point, even Ace and Peter had stopped talking to each other. Peter had new representation, Ace had his financial advisors, and getting things done was like pulling teeth.

> There is **always** a financial price to pay for getting off too early. Unfortunately, **you** are the only one left holding the bill.

For most of the end of the Farewell Tour, Peter decided to paint a tear running down his cheek over his KISS make-up. This was his very public announcement that he wasn't happy. Although he was happy enough to play with us onstage and get paid. We all were.

By the end of the American and South American tour, Peter gave us a take-it-or-leave-it demand for further and additional cash payments. We had Australia and Japan yet to do. We decided not to give in to any more pressure or blackmail—take your pick. We left it. We took Eric Singer instead, put on the Cat make-up and off we went. The kick-off concert was at Tokyo Stadium in Japan in front of fifty thousand screaming fans. Peter had shot himself in

To Gene!
You will always be the true God of Thunder!!
The Demon
WCW 2000

## THE DEMON

WCW.COM

© 2000 World Championship Wrestling, Inc. A Time Warner Company. All Rights Reserved

In 2000, I saw the enormous success of wrestling. For years I had been telling our legal people to send letters to various wrestlers to cease and desist using similar make-up. It became clearer and clearer to me that wrestling had simply become a KISS show. The characters wore outfits and, even though they wrestled, the intros to the events were pure KISS. The pyro came right out of our shows.

We went down to New Orleans to be on the Superbowl TV extravaganza. While we were there I tracked down Linda and Vince McMahon, the owners and founders of World Wrestling Federation (later Entertainment). I invited them down and in my hotel room we started talking about KISS wrestlers. My idea was there would be a Demon—a guy who had "been to hell and back." And the Starchild, who looked real pretty. Everyone wanted to beat him, but because of his athletic skills no one could touch him.

Eventually there would be the female versions: Lady Demon and Wild Child, and Cat Girl and even Space Girl. They would be gorgeous, of course, and no one would know what they looked like.

Eventually, both groups of wrestlers would meet and one of the couples might even have KISS Kids! Little kids in make-up.

Linda and Vince loved the idea. We started to negotiate right then and there. I told them I would get back to them. In the meantime, I also spoke with their competition, WCW, and they simply offered a better deal. We signed with them.

The Demon was born.

the foot. Yet again. The only thing he was successful at was preventing himself from getting millions of additional dollars. He had missed our debut Australian Tour in 1980 due to poor health reasons (self-abuse), and here he was again in the same boat.

By the end of the Farewell Tour in 2001, the band dispersed for some well-needed rest. Some of us significantly increased our bottom line (money) and some of us didn't. We could have all ridden the gravy train to the last stop. Some of us decided not to. There is always a financial price to pay for getting off too early. Unfortunately, you are the only one left holding the bill.

*       *       *

Even though we had been off tour for over a year, offers kept coming in. We kept declining. But two offers came in that looked promising. One was to play at a private function in Jamaica for a substantial fee, and the other offer was to play at the Olympics in Denver for no fee.

The legal people and our manager made numerous calls to Ace to join us for these two shows. I personally called and spoke with him on more than one occasion to ask him to play with us. He belonged on stage with us, I told him. He refused. He said he had his own career to worry about—that he was in the studio recording his solo album and that he already had numerous multi-million dollar offers to sign a solo record deal. He couldn't stop recording just to play with us, he said. It would interfere with his solo career.

I begged him to at least take two days off on the weekend to join us for the Olympics—where three billion people would see us. He agreed—with the proviso that we buy his guitar a seat next to him on the jet!

He played "Rock and Roll All Nite" with us at the Olympics for no fee, but refused to join us in Jamaica for a large fee.

The decisions you make for yourself either make you more money, or less.

Just last year, right before I went off to Australia to start my Lecture Tour, we got an offer to be involved in a KISS Symphony. The Melbourne Symphony Orchestra would team up with the band in front of thirty thousand people at Telstra Stadium (Melbourne Stadium). It would eventually become a pay-per-view and a live CD recording.

Peter had rejoined us. He was back with the family. He is a changed man. He shows up on time, bright and cheerful. He seems happy. And it's infectious. He has trained and worked hard and the results speak for themselves: he's never sounded better, drumming and singing. The fans are thrilled. So is the band.

As I sit here writing this we are two days away from the Symphony Stadium concert and everyone, especially Peter, is jazzed. It's actually a kick in the pants to hear him say things like, "You gotta enjoy every day. This is special. These memories will stay with us forever. No one can take that away from us."

This is the kind of clarity I have never heard from Peter before. It reminds me that despite the ups and downs, blood is thicker than water. Family is family.

And Ace? I have called him and heard nothing. I even flew in to surprise him at his birthday party. I gave him a birthday cake in front of his fans (it was a "private party"—one had to buy tickets to attend). I'm not sure it went down well with him. Something is bothering Ace and always has been. He has always tried to figure out what that "something" is—legally, personally, and in other ways. But so far, it has eluded him. He has a perennial dark cloud over his head. He may have put it there himself. We hope he'll be here. But unfortunately for Ace, whether he's there or not, the train will continue to roll.

We then go to Japan for three sold out in advance shows at the famed Budokan Colisuem. And then we play in Yokohama, due to overwhelming demand. The KISS lineup this time: Peter Criss on drums, Paul Stanley on guitar and vocals, myself and...Tommy Thayer on lead guitar. Ace Frehley has, unfortunately, shot himself in the foot yet again. Every decade or so, he figures out a way to hurt himself like no one else can. Unfortunate. Because Ace's absence will not only hurt himself, but the fans as well.

And yet, despite what Ace or anyone else might think, KISS can and will go on without him. It has before. It will again. No one member will dictate what the band will do. No one member is more important than the band itself. No...not even Paul or me. I believe KISS can continue without either or both of us.

Will Ace be back? Probably. Will he be welcome? Absolutely. Family is forever. But family will not stand still while one member decides to take some time off.

We are about to embark on a brand-new chapter of our career. We are now off Universal Records, where we had the largest record catalog—thirty-three albums released in the United States, and over forty albums released overseas. I have recently been able to negotiate successfully our own label deal—KISS Records. We will finally be master of our own fate. And there will be a DVD division as well—KISS DVD.

And if that weren't enough, we are about to embark on a worldwide tour with our friends Aerosmith, which promises to be the tour of the year.

And the future? There'll be lots of it. You bet. KISS is gearing up to do more great things. Greater than even I suspect. And as we have always said, we couldn't do it without you.

# CHAPTER NINE

# Rules of the Tongue

**A**s 2002 came and went, I noticed I had a lot more time to do the things I always wanted to do. KISS had been all-consuming. It continues to be. I am in the middle of negotiating a new deal for us: KISS World Stores. It may start in another country and eventually make its way here. I came up with the idea of KISS Kondoms, found a manufacturer, negotiated a joint venture and off we went. I seduced another comic book company, Dark Horse, to do a new line of KISS comics and negotiated the major points. We would own the comic book art. There were also KISS Kaskets and new KISS Action Figures.

But, for every successful venture I got us into, there were many that never saw the light of day. The ones that didn't succeed took as much time and effort as the ones that did. Nothing is easy. Again, if it were, everyone would do it.

I got close to a KISS Cartoon Show—funded by a Japanese company I found. I then combined them with a Canadian company, and we even went as far as getting contracts signed. But it never happened. Not yet, anyway.

I did succeed in getting the motion picture *Detroit Rock City* made (New Line). But

> **The ones that didn't succeed took as much time and effort as the ones that did. Nothing is easy. Again, if it were, everyone would do it.**

instead of being happy that we had our own movie, there were discussions internally about how much money everyone thought they were due, all the way to objections about my getting Producer credit.

I have a development slate of motion pictures and television shows that would rival most studios. But whether they ever see the light of day doesn't really matter. It costs me nothing (remember, I don't use staff or pay rent), and I work night and day at what I love doing.

*By 1999 I had produced New Line Pictures' Detroit Rock City. That experience opened up a brand-new world for me. The world of film had its own set of rules—decidedly different in tone from the "shoot from the hip" rock-and-roll world. For one thing, movie people tended to be well read and had a good work ethic. Had it not been for the guitar hanging around their necks, rock-and-roll was populated, let's be honest here, by people who would otherwise be asking you if you wanted fries with that.*

*The corporate structure at a movie studio was also different than a record company. For one thing, as a "Record Producer" I was in fact the "director" of the goings-on in a recording studio. As a "Movie Producer" I was the one who nurtured the material/script I wanted made into a movie, shopped it at a studio, negotiated the deal, and did whatever I had to do to keep the ship floating. The "Movie Director" actually wound up on the set fashioning the movie, in the same way that a "Record Producer" fashioned the record. So the language was different, the people were different and "stardom" in the music world held no sway in the movie world. A movie star means nothing in the music world; and in some ways being a star in the music world was a detriment to any kind of credibility in the movie world.*

*I had met President of Production for New Line Mike De Luca at a previous meeting. We were trying to figure out how to do a KISS movie. I had read a few ideas that just didn't grab me. One of them had to do with rock-and-roll being outlawed in the future. In the bowels of the underworld there existed a group of people who listened to and loved the "forbidden music" of KISS. You can guess where this was going. As it happened, they were living under Cobo Hall in Detroit. Needless to say, that idea didn't go far.*

*I then met Barry Levine, who had been the band's photographer in the 70s. He was shopping a movie of the week for television. The idea was about fans of the band and how they were going to have to surmount all sorts of difficulties to get to Detroit to see their band. He was shopping this television movie without me knowing about it. When I found out I called and explained to him that he couldn't mount the movie without our permission, since we owned certain "underlying rights" like the make-up, the logo and so on. Besides, if the idea was so good, why not shop it to a movie studio? It could still wind up as a tv movie in reruns.*

*That was the history of Detroit Rock City. But I had many other ideas for movies, and De Luca was receptive. Writer Jeph Loeb (who I first worked with when we tossed around an idea as a starring vehicle for me, later to star Arnold Schwarzenegger, in a movie called* Commando*) came over to my house and we started talking about movies. He and I shared a love of horror*

**The Hollywood Reporter**

*LATIN MUSIC SPECIAL ISSUE*

Who's who in Hollywood — page 76

*George Christy's* **The Great Life**

69th year · June 18-20, 1999 · $1.85 (California) $2.65 (Elsewhere)

*a BPi publication*

## Fox moves give Hill's duties to Chernin, Carey

**By Stephen Battaglio and Lynette Rice**

Fox executives said Thursday that they don't plan to replace David Hill when he relinquishes his role as chairman and CEO of Fox Broadcasting to a new entity that will oversee Fox's sports media interests around the world.

It was widely speculated News Corp. co-chairman and chief operating officer Chernin considered replacing with 20th Century Fox Television president Sandy Grushow wanted a new, position putting him in charge of television operations at Instead, the former Fox entertainment Group president

*See HILL on page*

*Grushow*

## A new boo-boo for Katzenberg

**By David Robb**

Jeffrey Katzenberg's expert witness has acknowledged making another mistake in calculating the value of Katzenberg's disputed bonus — a $143 million accounting error that will raise the size of Katzenberg's 2% bonus by nearly $3 million.

It's the third error that Mr. J. Wolf has acknowledged making

*See KATZENBERG on page*

## 'Dadd long le

It looks lil another b winner fo Adam San ler. Review on page 10.

*Sandler*

# Uni's Mulligan, Snider get green light at studio

**By Zorianna Kit**

Brian Mulligan and Stacey Snider have been promoted to co-chairmen of Universal Pictures, it was announced Thursday. The appointments were expected (HR 5/24).

The promotions leave Kevin Misher as co-president of production. Misher, who has been reporting to Snider since he joined Universal in February 1996, is expected to be bumped up to sole production president imminently. Reps for Universal declined comment.

Snider and Mulligan's promotions fill a vacuum that has been in place since Casey Silver resigned as chairman of the department in November and Chris McGurk exited as president of Universal

*Mulligan* · *Snider*

Pictures to become vice chairman of MGM in April.

They also acknowledge a turnaround taking place in Universal's movie lineup after a woeful run that saw disappointments including "Mercury Rising," "Black Dog," "Fear and Loathing in Las Vegas," "Babe: Pig in the City" and "Meet Joe Black."

Universal has recently benefited from the boxoffice success of such films as "The Mummy," "Life" and

*See UNIVERSAL on page 74*

---

**The Hollywood Reporter** · www.hollywoo[d]

## Simmons

*Continued from page 1—*

Titled "Real Monsters," the pitch is described as "Abbott and Costello Meet Frankenstein" and "The Ghost and Mr. Chicken." The story will follow two buffoonish dock workers who open the wrong crate during the graveyard shift and inadvertently release three hideously horrifying monsters into the New York City night. Fearing the loss of their jobs, the skittish workers have to figure out a way to get the monsters back in their box, while trying to remain alive themselves.

"Movies like 'Abbott and Costello Meet Frankenstein' were chiller comedies that were both extremely funny and extremely scary," Simmons said. "We want to re-create a similar spirit with two brand new characters in a movie that will hopefully turn into a franchise."

"I'm ecstatic to be working with New Line Cinema and Gene Simmons for a second time," Rifkin said. "Making 'Detroit Rock City' together was a blast. 'Real Monsters' is right up my alley ... Combining laughs and scares for the same creative team as 'Detroit Rock City' is a dream come true."

Simmons will produce "Monsters" with Jeph Loeb, marking the rocker's third project for New Line through his Gene Simmons Co. His

*Simmons* · *Rifkin*

"Groupies" — about two girls whose humdrum lives are changed by the arrival of a rock band in their small town — is being written by Allison Anders and Kurt Voss.

New Line senior vp production Brian Witten will oversee "Monsters" with production president Michael De Luca.

"We had such a great time working with Adam and Gene on 'Detroit Rock City,' we were eager to get back into business with them again," De Luca said.

Rifkin, who is repped by the William Morris Agency and manager Brad Wyman, wrote such films as "MouseHunt" and "Small Soldiers." Directorial credits include "Denial" and "The Chase" — both from his own scripts — as well as the mockumentary feature "Welcome to Hollywood."

Loeb, also credited as Joseph Loeb III, is a writer/producer whose credits include "Burglar," "Teen Wolf" and "Commando." □

*MORE THAN EVER, THE QUALITY SHOWS*

## NL rocking on with Simmons

**By Zorianna Kit**

Following a successful collaboration on the upcoming New Line Cinema feature "Detroit Rock City," the studio is back in business with the film's producer, Kiss founder Gene Simmons, and director Adam Rifkin.

The studio has purchased a comedy-horror pitch from Simmons that Rifkin will write and direct as his next project.

*See SIMMONS on page 74*

## CTTG primed for ATG's programs

**By Lynette Rice**

Columbia TriStar Television Group announced Thursday that it will distribute primetime shows produced by Artists Television Group — the new unit of Mike Ovitz's Artists Management Group.

At the same time, CTTG said

*See AMG on page 73*

---

movies and of comedy. And, we both loved Abbott and Costello Meet Frankenstein. *Well, we mused, what would happen if* Dumb and Dumber *met "Monsters?" I called* Detroit Rock City *director Adam Rifkin (who had already written* Toy Soldiers *and* Mousehunt*) and asked if he would write and direct* Real Monsters, *our proposed movie. With Adam onboard, Jeph and I pitched De Luca, who bought the project in the room. When Jeph left, I stayed behind to tell De Luca about another idea I had called* Groupies, *about two girls and their rites of passage when they meet a rock band. He bought that one too.*

The Gene Simmons Company *was alive and on the map. In quick succession I sold* Sex Drugs and Rock 'n' Roll *to the Disney company as a starring vehicle for Jim Carrey;* The Neal Bogart Story *to Paramount;* Jon Sable *(based on the comic strip) to Pacifica;* November Files *and* Tennessee Waltz *to Interlight;* Rock and Roll All Nite *to CBS as a movie of the week; and* My Dad the Rock Star, *a cartoon show I created, to Nelvana. I had another twenty to thirty other projects set up at various other places.*

The astonishing thing about the movie industry is that there is a real wall between a movie that is "developed" (scripts written, fees paid) and a movie that is shot (filmed).

Records are different. If you have a record deal, the record will come out. I had lots of movie deals, but none of these projects have ever been released as of yet.

There's always tomorrow!

LIBERTY PICTURES
- LOGO -
Gene (signed)
JAN 30 · 2002

# LIBERTY
## PICTURES

IN CASE NAME CLEARS
HERE'S THE IDEA!!
— Gene

For about a year now, my partners and I have been in heavy discussions with investment people about starting a new film/television company to produce and release motion pictures, using existing movie companies to distribute. We had to come up with a name.

I tend to think visually and liked Paramount's "mountain" logo. But the most memorable movie logo was certainly MGM's lion. I focused in on the Statue of Liberty. I had read that no one actually owned its image and that you could only trademark the Statue of Liberty logo within the context of your reference.

I also liked the name Liberty Films. It sounded big and free. I thought it would be appealing to filmmakers, because it didn't have restrictions. It implied the filmmaker would have the freedom to be creative.

I drew the logo at the Plaza Hotel in New York and faxed it to my lawyers. It didn't clear. There was a Liberty Pictures already in existence and, I found out, the original Liberty Pictures was owned by Frank Capra, the director of one of my favorite films, It's A Wonderful Life.

We are currently toying with "Sanctuary Pictures," which we own. I came up with the name—I thought it would make creative people feel that our company would be a sanctuary from the cold business world. I found out there is an existing Sanctuary Group. It engages in music management and is a record company. Instead of trying to come up with another name, I thought I would contact them and see if they objected to my using Sanctuary as a name for motion pictures. It was an area they were not active in, and, if there wasn't a competitive use of the name, perhaps they wouldn't object.

They didn't. They were nice enough to give us a letter stating that they had no objection and that I could own "Sanctuary Pictures." This meant my partners and I could "greenlight" (approve a script to be shot). It's the kind of power few people on the planet wield. The ones who do are called moguls.

We are in the final stages of financing. When and if we get funded, the name of our motion picture company is going to be Sanctuary Pictures.

Fingers crossed.

*My Dad the Rock Star* (Nelvana) is a cartoon show I cocreated that has just started production.

I got close on more than one occasion at having a KISS Broadway play produced. I brought on the producer/choreographer of *The Lion King* and the writer of *Hedwig and the Angry Inch*. Financing never came. Not yet, anyway.

The KISS Comics deal with Dark Horse is morphing into additional characters. I came up with the idea of a "Mr. Speed" and a "Christine 16" comics series. It will kick off in KISS Comics and then launch into its own title. There have already been conversations about a host of characters, and we will take them one at a time.

But while KISS was and continues to be immensely time-consuming and satisfying, I was also always interested in launching the Gene Simmons brand. I designed, built and marketed my own line of bass guitars—the Gene Simmons *Axe* Bass and the Gene Simmons *Punisher*. I arranged for the manufacturing, shipping, and marketing in the same way as I did with the *Kisstory* books. They have both been huge sellers. I am currently negotiating with a guitar company to make them available in every music store.

I wrote my autobiography for Crown Books—*Kiss and Make-Up*. It became a *New York Times* best-seller. The paperback edition recently came out and is already on its way to becoming another best-seller. As an aside, when Crown was telling me their plans for the paperback edition, I strongly urged them to do four separate covers for the collectors. They seemed perplexed by the idea. I told them to trust me and, using their language, explained that it would make them more money. They liked that part.

I urged them to give me my own imprint—Simmons Books. The idea was they would pay for all expenses and we would split profits. They didn't go for the deal.

So I met Michael Viner at New Millennium Press (publisher of the Stephen Hawking book, the Bill Maher book, Bob Evans's *The*

The music industry, and most industries in general, have "smoke walls" in between them. For example, if you're a recording artist you would usually have a recording company, a record producer, a distribution system and so on. Almost without exception, these are always different entities and every one of these entities wants to get paid—by you. The recording artist, in essence, pays the record company (not the other way around) and everyone else, including the store, to manufacture and distribute his records.

But what would happen if the recording artist were the record company and the distribution company and so on? Wouldn't he make more money per unit sold? Because the record industry deals in millions of records and because the United States and the rest of the world is so big, that scenario doesn't make sense, simply because of the massive scale.

But a musician and his instrument are another matter. The musician either buys or "endorses" a guitar he uses. The guitars are sold in stores and cost a lot of money. The music industry (and most industries) work in the following way. First, there is the "price of goods" (what it actually costs in manpower and manufacturing/distribution costs to produce a product—in this case a guitar). Then the manufacturer, say Wombat Guitars (who, incidentally, would actually manufacture their guitars overseas in China, North Korea and other places that don't have union pay or union rules—i.e., it's far cheaper, even with shipping costs) adds on a profit for themselves. They then sell the guitar to a distributor or store, who in turn doubles the price of the instrument to reach the eventual "sale price."

The actual price to manufacture a bass guitar? Anywhere from $200 to $300 per instrument (if actually manufactured overseas) for decent quality. Then tack on a profit for the company, which sells it to the store for $750. The store in turn doubles the sale price to $1,500 per instrument when you buy it. Sometimes even more.

The store makes $750 profit per instrument (but remember, they have rent and staff to pay for). Wombat Guitar Company makes about $500 profit per instrument (but remember, they have rent and staff to pay for).

I studied the business model and wondered why I couldn't become the manufacturer, distributor, "store" and recording artist all in one. In other words, if I could cut out all the middlemen and assume all financial risk (which would be minimal, since I would simply wait for orders to come in and manufacture only for cash on hand), wouldn't I stand to make the lion's share of profit per instrument?

CUT THE

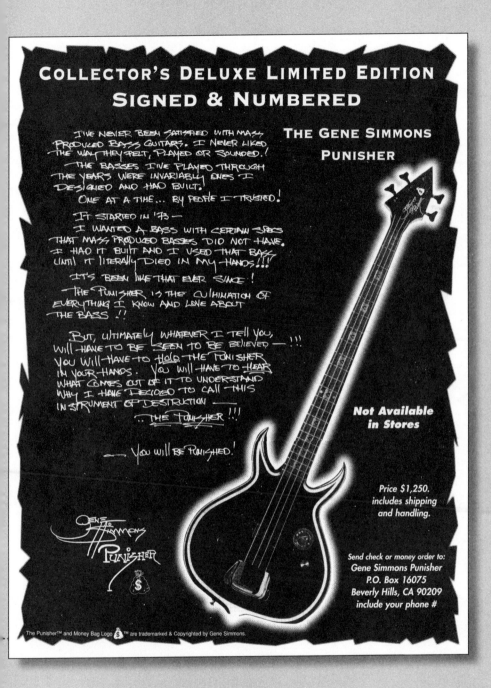

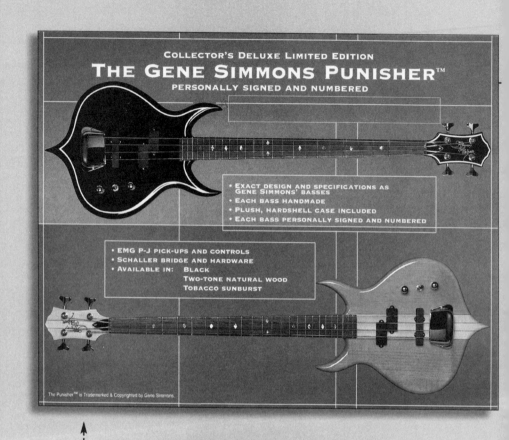

COLLECTOR'S DELUXE LIMITED EDITION
# THE GENE SIMMONS PUNISHER™
PERSONALLY SIGNED AND NUMBERED

- EXACT DESIGN AND SPECIFICATIONS AS GENE SIMMONS' BASSES
- EACH BASS HANDMADE
- PLUSH, HARDSHELL CASE INCLUDED
- EACH BASS PERSONALLY SIGNED AND NUMBERED

- EMG P-J PICK-UPS AND CONTROLS
- SCHALLER BRIDGE AND HARDWARE
- AVAILABLE IN:   BLACK
                  TWO-TONE NATURAL WOOD
                  TOBACCO SUNBURST

The Punisher™ is Trademarked & Copyrighted by Gene Simmons.

# GHER PROFIT

*I tried to make deals with guitar companies in the early 80s for a Gene Simmons Axe (a name I also trademarked). A few hundred were made. I signed every one. I netted about $100 profit per instrument—times 250 pieces, that equaled $25,000. Not bad, I thought. But, I could do better. The trouble was, I didn't know the business model.*

*In the mid-90s I had the time and the intention to do it myself. I designed and trademarked "The Gene Simmons Punisher." Marvel Comics already had a "Punisher" comic book character, and they objected to my use of the name. They also implied a lawsuit would be forthcoming if I continued. I thought I had a good chance of winning the case, so after a few conversations with my legal counsel Marvel, to their credit, acquiesced (they let me go ahead, without challenge).*

*I started with a handwritten note assuring everyone I would sign and number every instrument. The quality would be top-notch. This was a bass I would personally use live. I circulated the flyer to all the fanzines. I did a mailing to some of the fans. They, in turn, circulated it to their friends. The actual marketing (or promotion) costs were a few hundred dollars. The initial price of the Punisher bass was $1,250, but soon rose to $1,500 and then to $3,000.*

*I distributed the bass through the mail. You sent your check and I mailed the bass straight to you.*

*I then reintroduced my Gene Simmons Axe bass. The same successful business model was applied. This time I not only sold my Axe and Punisher basses through the mail, I also sold about a thousand to Spencer Gift stores. I continued to make my normal profit.*

*The fans were happy because they received the highest quality. They received personalized attention. If anyone wrote about a defect in the basses, I personally arranged to either replace or fix it. No waiting in line. No corporate shuffling.*

*If I would have done it the original way, I would have made $500,000. That's certainly a respectable figure. However, with my business model and a little more work on my part, I was able to reap a much higher profit with very little financial risk.*

*Working hard = making more money.*

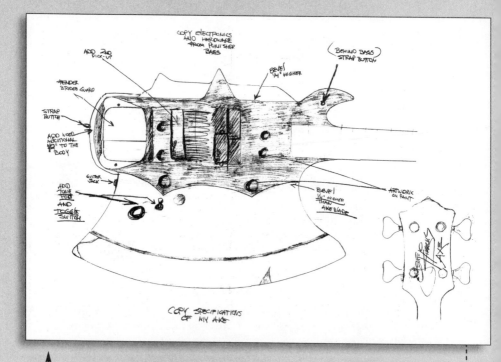

The Gene Simmons Axe came about because I've always been interested in language. Especially slang. Most American slang comes from African-Americans. American musical slang comes from jazz and blues musicians.

I've always heard musicians refer to their guitars as their "Axe." I liked the sound of it, but never knew why guitars were axes. Because I came from another country, I tended to visualize words, as in "hot dog." For years I would see a sweating dog in my mind. It's a strange (not necessarily appetizing) reference to frankfurters (originally from Frankfurt, Germany, actually).

Every musician knew what "Axe" meant. I wondered if anyone actually owned the word. I applied to the Trademark Office and was surprised to receive ownership. It means no one else can have a guitar or bass and refer to it as an Axe (as a name for the instrument).

And then I wondered why my bass shouldn't actually look like an axe. It would certainly fit with my Demon persona. I had never designed a bass before. I knew nothing about the marketplace and its demands. I just knew what I liked. And through the years, trusting what I like has served me well. I designed what I liked and sent it into the Trademark Office (to make sure another guitar company couldn't use my design). I was surprised to not only receive a trademark for my design, but also have it also designated as an "invention." I invented something.

I used commercial pickups—EMGs (the bass's built in "microphone") and a pick guard from Fender Music Man basses. I then found a Korean manufacturer who manufactured basses for American guitar companies. I ordered and paid for only the number of basses that were prepaid. That way, my financial exposure was minimal and my profit, a continuing stream. If I over-produced the instrument, I would, in effect, be in the storage business (paying for housing the unsold basses).

The Gene Simmons Axe first debuted on the Creatures of the Night tour in 1982.

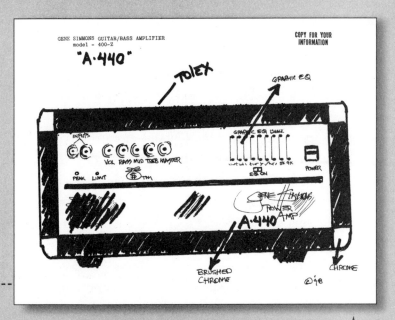

Most things take a long time.

Around the same time I was selling the Punisher and Axe basses, I thought I might as well have a Gene Simmons Bass Amplifier out there as well. For well over two decades I had been using AMPEG SVT bass amplifiers. They were very road-worthy. They had enormous power (360 watts rms versus a Marshall amplifier, which had 100 watts) and they looked powerful. Each cabinet had two fifteen-foot speakers. I used eight cabinets and amplifiers stacked up on top of each other.

I had started doing amplifier "endorsements" with Ampeg—usually along the lines of "Gene Simmons uses Ampegs." But it occurred to me in return for getting my picture in a magazine, the company was making money and I was not.

So I called a guy who worked for the company and who had coincidentally been in a band we originally opened for. Ken Hensley had been the keyboard player in a British group called Uriah Heep. KISS opened for them in 1975 in Indianapolis. Within six months, when we returned to the same arena, Heep was opening for KISS. Hensley eventually left the band and started working for St. Louis Music, which owned Ampeg. So when he and I started talking about a Gene Simmons Amplifier, we both understood what was needed.

I wanted an amplifier strong enough for bass players to use, but with enough clarity for a guitar player. Eventually, we settled on the Gene Simmons Punisher Amplifier as a name tag. I designed the amplifier (which I called the "A-440" after the A-440 number on an electronic tuning machine, which told you if you were in tune. If you read any number other than the A-440, you were out of tune.). Notice the "moneybag" logo under the "bass" and "mid" knobs.

Less than one hundred amplifiers were manufactured and sold.

That attempt was around 1995. It's now 2003, and I'm finalizing a new round of Gene Simmons Bass Amplifiers through Ampeg. This time the business structure is more sound and the amp looks like it's going to be a huge smash based on preorders.

If at first you don't succeed...

*Kid Stays in the Picture* book and audiobook), and he and I decided to team up. Voila!! Simmons Books/New Millennium Press.

The debut volume of my imprint is in your hands: *Sex Money Kiss*. And, lest we forget about no stone being left unturned: Simmons Audio/New Millennium Audio is my talking book imprint, debuting with the powerful and attractive Gene Simmons reading his own *Kiss and Make-Up* in an eight-CD box set. I was able to get Crown Books to give me the audio rights without a fee being paid. Thank you.

I started my own magazine, *GENE SIMMONS TONGUE*—a joint venture with Allen Tuller's Sterling MacFadden publishing house. As I sit here writing this, the fourth issue with Jack Nicholson on the cover is just hitting the stands. In case you've been living in a cave the past year, it's the smash hit of the magazine world. Wanna subscribe? Go to any newsstand or go to genesimmonstongue.com.

And genesimmons.com is my home. I log on daily, if I can. I post news. I answer mail and, most importantly, some of the most beautiful women in the world keep sending me their photos for our "Ladies in Waiting" section. Log on.

I am negotiating for the opening of the first Gene Simmons Store, a general pop culture store. It's a slow process, but it will see the light of day shortly.

I have, quite by accident, become a successful lecturer. UCLA asked me to lecture at the Business School, then I was asked to speak at a music conference in Vancouver. Then the University of Florida asked me to lecture. And then, Madison Entertainment out of Australia asked if I would consider coming Down Under for a Lecture Tour! I came, I lectured. I filmed and recorded everything. It will see the light of day as a book, a DVD and whatever else I can think of—all on Simmons Books and Simmons Audio.

# WANTED TO START MY OWN MAGAZINE

My relationship with the publisher of the KISS SPECIAL magazines continued through the years and its head, Allen Tuller, became someone I could look to as a friend instead of as a foe. Over the years the phone calls evolved into one particular conversation I had with him. I wanted to start my own magazine. I wasn't sure what it should be, but I was sure what it shouldn't be. I didn't want nudity, although I wanted lots of pretty girls. The nudity issue simply had to do with being relegated to one area of the magazine racks, right next to Big Hooters magazine. I'd rather be next to Time magazine.

It's the same point of view I had with the original Marvel Comics when they first wanted to do a KISS Comic back in the 70s. They wanted to do a traditional comic book. I rejected that, not because I didn't love comics. I did. It's simply that as a comic book, it would be placed right next to all the other comic books. And not all the fans go to the comic book rack. Most of them stand in front of the general magazine rack. I pushed Marvel to do a comic magazine—a comic book that was the same size and priced the same as regular magazines. In point of fact, even if the newsstand wanted to rack it along with the other comic books, it couldn't. The KISS comic/mag was too big to fit into a comic book slot. Marvel was nervous about a $1.50 KISS comic when comics of the time sold for twenty-five or thirty-five cents. I was confident. Our comic became Marvel's biggest seller—at four times the price of a regular comic!

Market research is something professionals look to as an indication of whether it's a good time or not to enter the marketplace. And yet at a time when donut shops were doing terrible business, Krispy Kreme donuts exploded. At a time when rock-and-roll was bland, KISS exploded. My opinion has always been that, despite the times, there is always a demand for something good. There will always be a demand, in good times and in bad times, for something people want. That's obvious.

I originally wanted a magazine that was a cross between Rolling Stone (although without the embarrassing political commentary by college students) and Playboy (without the nudity). Actually, the tone of the magazine I wanted to do felt closer to Playboy than to Rolling Stone. I wanted to do a "lifestyle" magazine. A magazine that would be an extension of who I am—in the same way Playboy is actually Hugh Hefner.

My philosophy about life has always been upfront. I've never been married. I'm not familiar with the term, actually. I have never been willing to hide my attraction to all living females of the species. Any other behavior on my part (or on the part of any other healthy, hetero male) is a lie.

So what should the magazine be called? I suggested GROUPIES. "The bands and the girls who love them." I half believed in the idea. I tried to make myself believe in it. I have always loved groupies.

In society, before a guy can become intimate with a girl, he has to wine and dine her, talk to her (a lot) and eventually, if she finds him charming, funny and is sure he is not seeing any other females at that time, she might share his bed with him. He has to be willing to jump through many hoops before he can play with his bone.

Now, rock-and-roll or, more specifically, being in a rock band is proof positive that God exists. Because in that arena, the woman's rules don't apply. She will be there ready and willing to have sex with a guy she has never met. He will not have to talk much (the male of the species doesn't do that—unless he's a hairdresser). He will not have to take her to dinner. He will not settle down with her. She will not be the only female he will be with (perhaps even that evening!). She will not be allowed to ask him where he's going or who he's been with. The reply might be, "Who wants to know?" In fact, he might never ask her what her name is!

And yet the "primal honesty of it all" is right there. He wants her. She wants him. Period. No strings attached. If she goes back to the hotel with him, they can do the encores together. Will he ever see her again? It's up to him. Is she allowed to call and torture him with lines like "Where is this all going?" Or, "What did this mean to you?" Answer: No.

So, it seemed like a good idea. Tuller's response was that it sounded limiting. If this was to be a magazine as an extension of who I am, then why not call it GENE SIMMONS magazine (like Oprah magazine). I suggested GENE SIMMONS TONGUE. We both loved it.

I could pick up the phone and have access to other celebs, so we didn't need anyone with that cachet. But who would be our premier cover person? Should we do a Maxim and go with a pretty girl? Tuller put together a few cover layout ideas featuring Rachael Leigh Cook (an actress), and I sat down and tried to design our cover logo.

We fooled around with different logos for GENE SIMMONS TONGUE. At the end of the day there's no right or wrong. It's all about taste, perhaps.

But there is also the consideration that above and beyond what I liked, did the logo and/or cover give the impression we wanted to give.

The Jamie Presley example of a cover didn't work for me. I also didn't like the logo. It looked too feminine to me. If there was to be an actress on the cover, how she posed and what she was wearing would have a lot to do with the impression you were getting. I preferred the Rachael Leigh Cook cover idea. I believe that beauty and sexuality lie in the eyes of a woman, contrary to what you might think. The photo of Cook is direct. Her eyes tell you everything. I don't need to see her boobs. The logo, now less feminine, looked too "college" for me.

GENE SIMMONS TONGUE would show no nudity. This was a pragmatic decision, as I said before. If we didn't show nudity, we wouldn't be relegated to the section of the newsstand devoted to those kinds of magazines, and most stores wouldn't have a problem displaying us.

The further we went in the process, the more nervous I got that the cover had to be something else. So I sat down and started doodling. I drew Hugh Hefner's head in the middle and surrounded him with girls—designed to look like a flower, with Hef in the middle. I faxed Hef the cover idea and asked him if he would honor me with being the cover person of my debut issue. It only took him a day or two to get back to me and agree.

GENE SIMMONS TONGUE magazine was born!

GENE SIMMONS TONGUE

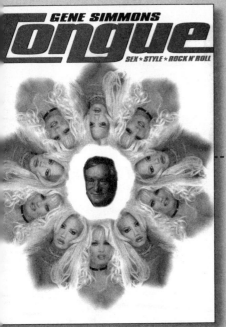

COVER IDEA

EF.

DEC 27·01

WOULD BE HONORED TO HAVE YOU ON OUR 1ST ISSUE COVER!!

JOINT VENTURE WITH STERLING, McFADDEN!!!

T ISSUE ON SALE APRIL '02.

NUDITY.!!

0,000 PRINT ORDER.

(ALL THE GIRLS HAVE THEIR TONGUES OUT)

TONGUE LASHINGS" - LETTER COLUMN

TONGUE IN CHEEK" - GOSSIP!!

FORKED TONGUE" - FOOD

... AND SO ON

I am finalizing possibly the biggest potential deal I have ever been involved with. I have the most professional partners and I am in the midst of an investment consortium that's about to fund a Movie-Television-Entertainment company.

I have a deal with the television program *Extra* on NBC for one-on-one interviews, also providing me with an opportunity to promote my books and magazines on national television.

You may be thinking to yourself that the above is blatantly self-serving. Precisely.

I remember hearing Cassius Clay, who became Mohammed Ali, first declare himself as "The Greatest." He would yell, "I am the prettiest. I am the best fighter that has ever existed." People thought he was boasting. He was simply telling the truth.

## I say humble be damned.

If you're not willing to tell anyone and everyone who and what you are, you may lose. Advertise yourself. You are your own best product. You know yourself better than anyone does. Or, at least you should. Remember in school they taught us, "Know thyself."

YOU are your own biggest potential for reaping the rewards life has to offer. YOU will either make more money or less, completely depending on what decisions you make for yourself.

This is not a "Ten-Step Easy Course to Riches" book. They tend not to work. Neither do diets. I'm sure you've noticed. The only thing that works is YOU. What do YOU want to do with your life? How hard are YOU willing to work at getting what you want?

I'm not going to do very much for you if you want a paint-by-numbers list of what you should do once you finish my book. If I've succeeded in making you think for yourself, decide for yourself and, most importantly, think of yourself *first* (despite what society tells you), you may benefit financially.

And I can only address the financial issues. I'm not your shrink. I'm not your preacher or rabbi. Remember, I'm the guy who may not be qualified to do many things besides stick out his tongue...and yet I've done very well for myself. Better than most people on the face of the planet.

And the way I have done that and the way I continue to do that is to THINK FOR MYSELF. I stand by all my failures and I want all the credit for my successes. No excuses for failure, and certainly not an inch of humbleness anywhere near me for my successes.

## If I fail, I did it. ME. No one else.
## If I win, I did it. ME. No one else.

I was thinking of calling this book ME. I was told sex, money and even KISS had a more commercial sound to it. And yet ME is ultimately what it's all about. Yes, be kind. Yes, watch out for your loved ones. But I would urge you to get comfortable with the idea of ME. It should the single most important word you are concerned with.

And finally, my fondest wishes to you for wealth and happiness!

# Photograph Credits

## TEXT PHOTOGRAPHS:

Page iv (opposite page 1): Artwork by
© Spiro Papadatos/Spirographics 2003.
Photo by © David Safian 2002.

Page 9: Remo Camerota, Whitewall
Productions, Australia.

Page 85: Article reprinted with permission
of *New York Post.* © 2003 *New York
Post* Holdings Inc., d/b/a *New York Post.*

Page 94: Remo Camerota,
Whitewall Productions, Australia.

Page 103: *Runaway* © 1984 Tri-Star
Pictures, Inc. Courtesy of Tri-Star Pictures.

Page 108: ©VNU Business Media Inc.
Used with permission from *Billboard Magazine.*

Page 110: Article by Patrick Goldstein
originally published July 17, 1988.
Copyright 1988 *Los Angeles Times.*
Reprinted with permission.

Page 117: Dean Freeze,
Whitewall Productions, Australia.

Page 177: Remo Camerota,
Whitewall Productions, Australia.

Page 207: Remo Camerota,
Whitewall Productions, Australia.

Page 209: Reprinted with permission of
*The Hollywood Reporter.*

## COLOR PLATES:

*Detroit Rock City* © 1999, New Line
Productions, Inc. All rights reserved.
Poster appears courtesy of New Line
Productions, Inc.

*Time Out New York* cover reprinted with
permission of Time Out New York.

*New York Magazine* cover reprinted with
permission of *New York Magazine.*
Photo by Frank W. Ockenfels III.

*LA Weekly* cover reprinted with permission
of *LA Weekly.* Photo by Brooks Craft.

Cover image of *Folio®* magazine from the
April 2002 issue, used with permission.
Copyright 2002, Media Central Inc.,
a PRIMEDIA company. All rights reserved.

All Australian lecture tour photographs
by Remo Camerota and Dean Freeze,
Whitewall Productions, Australia.
Whitewall@itconnect.net.au

All other photographs and illustrations are
courtesy of the author.

# Index